THE NIGHT THE STARS SANG
The Wonder That Is Christmas

THE NIGHT THE STARS SANG
The Wonder That Is Christmas

Fleming H. Revell Company
and
Triumph™ Books
Tarrytown, New York

Triumph™ Books edition published by
special arrangement with Guideposts Books

Library of Congress Cataloging-in-Publication Data

The Night the stars sang : the wonder that is Christmas.
     p.   cm.
    Reprint. Originally published: Carmel, N.Y.: Guideposts, c1990.
    Includes index.
    ISBN 0-8007-3021-6
    1. Christmas.
  [GT4985.N52 1991]
  394.2′68282—dc20   91-11692
                                            CIP

Every attempt has been made to credit the sources of copyrighted material used in this book. If any such acknowledgment has been inadvertently omitted or miscredited, receipt of such information would be appreciated.

Photo and art credits and copyright permission notices appear on pages 190 and 191, and constitute an extension of the copyright page.

Produced in association with Welcome Enterprises, Inc.
164 East 95th Street, New York, New York 10128

Published by Triumph™ Books
An Imprint of Gleneida Publishing Group, Tarrytown, New York
Printed in the United States of America

The Editors wish to express special thanks to
Welcome Enterprises, Inc.
for their unique contribution in producing this book:

To Lena Tabori, Project Director,
for her highly original vision and commitment to
creating a book of beauty and excellence,
and for her masterful shepherding of this project.

To Linda Sunshine, Project Editor,
for her careful and sensitive fine-tuning and organizing
of the manuscript into its present form, and for her
expert personal touch in managing all aspects of the project.

Finally, to Michelle Wiener, Book Designer,
who brought charm, tenacity and a loving touch to each page
and to Judy Pelikan, whose cover and
musical chapter openings give this book its visual soul.

It has been a gift for all of us to have worked on this book and
we hope it is a gift to you, your family and friends.

The Editors

TABLE OF CONTENTS

CLASSIC CHRISTMAS STORIES

FAVORITE AND NEW CHRISTMAS STORIES

THE WONDER OF CHRISTMAS AND CHILDREN

FAMILY TRADITIONS AND HOMEMADE GIVING

VII

FAMILY CHRISTMAS MEALS AND RECIPES

WE WISH YOU A MERRY CHRISTMAS

INTRODUCTION

WE WISH YOU
A MERRY CHRISTMAS

Every year as Christmas draws near, a kind of breathless anticipation seems to creep over the world. A hushed expectancy. A growing sense of something tremendous about to happen. Reminding us that, one night long ago, even the stars sang out in a glorious tribute:

"Be glad. Be joyful. Be happy for a great
Gift is coming to you!"

It's not a gift you can see or touch or unwrap under the Christmas tree. It's far more precious. It's the indescribable sense of awe and wonder that comes when the celebration of Christ's birth reminds us once more that long ago God gave Himself to us in the form of a newborn Baby lying in a hay-filled manger.

How astonishing that is! And adding to the amazement and gratitude we feel is the knowledge that, if we let it, the Spirit of Christmas will come into our hearts and make a permanent home there, filling us with a deep and abiding love.

For most of us, there is a specific moment when we feel that Spirit of Christmas. Sounds can do it: the high, sweet voices of children singing carols in the night or the strains of Handel's *Messiah.* Aromas can do it: bayberry or cinnamon, chestnuts roasting on a busy street corner. Sights can do it: a tall tree glowing with lights, small noses pressed against cold windowpanes as the snow drifts down outside. Storytelling can do it, if the storyteller has the magical gift of enchantment. Prayer can do it, if you see a crèche somewhere and in your mind join the kneeling shepherds for a moment of silent adoration.

All around us at this time of year are the signs and symbols of Christmas. And in *The Night the Stars Sang* the joy and wonder of this magical and holy season are celebrated. Read about it in the wondrous miracle of that First Christmas; in the blessed prayers and poems to inspire your worship; in the family traditions and homemade giving to help prepare your hearts; in the beloved Christmas classics and the new Christmas stories by Sue Monk Kidd, Madeleine L'Engle, Norman Vincent Peale, Marilyn Morgan Helleberg, Arthur Gordon, Van Varner, Dina Donohue, and many more; in the warm stories and activities to enchant the hearts of children; and in the timeless Christmas recipes shared from festive tables.

This is our Christmas present to you. Share it with your children, your family, your friends. Feel the excitement grow. Let the wonder be upon you. Welcome the warmth of Bethlehem in your heart, as real and true today as it was so long ago on that holy night when the Savior was born, the night the stars sang.

The Editors

THE FIRST NOEL

CHAPTER

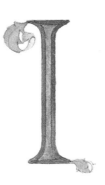

THE WAY TO THE FIRST CHRISTMAS

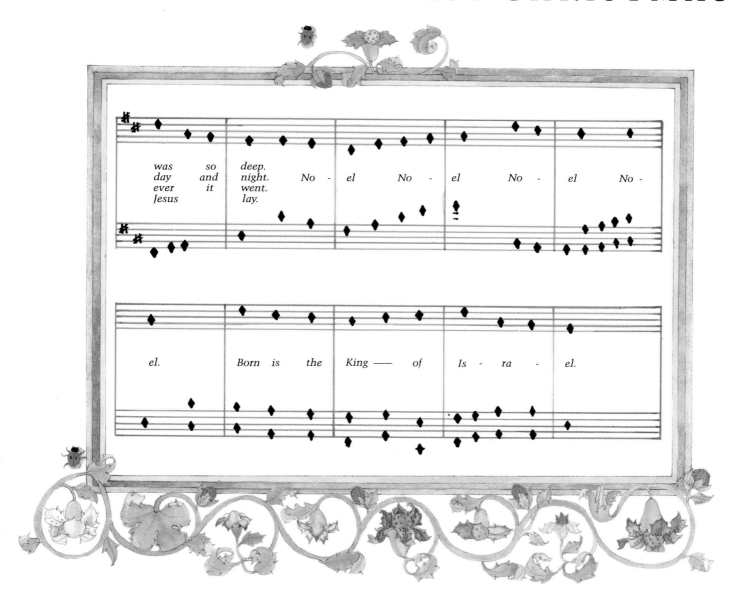

THE WAY TO
THE FIRST CHRISTMAS

Malachi Martin

And it came to pass in those days, that there went out a decree from Caesar Augustus that all the world should be taxed...

(Luke 2:1)

It is a matter of great urgency. As members of the tribe of Judah, Joseph and his wife Mary must register for the census in Bethlehem, their own ancestral city of David. The Romans, who occupy Palestine, are strict. Anyone not appearing at the appointed time will risk being branded an outlaw, fined, executed.

And there is the other reason. Mary is heavy with Child. The quickest way south must be chosen, not the easier plains of the Mediterranean or the more leisurely Jordan Valley, but the 3000-year-old trading route that winds for 70 miles through the rocky highlands.

Joseph purchases a place in a caravan passing through from Mesopotamia. It will provide protection from bandits, bears, mountain lions...

"The Way To The First Christmas" by Malachi Martin was first published in Guideposts Magazine and is reprinted by permission of the author. Text and map © by Malachi Martin Enterprises, Ltd.

DAY ONE

The long, cumbersome caravan leaves Nazareth in a welter of dust and yapping dogs, the rich in their chariots and wagons, the poor on donkeys and foot. As they descend from the high Galilean hills, Mary observes Mount Tabor in the east. She cannot know it now, but one day it will be the site of the Transfiguration of the Child she carries—the Child who will be called Jesus.

DAY TWO

The lovely plain of JEZREEL, Palestine's granary. Green forests, fresh water, carpets of wildflowers. Mary misses home. And sleeping on the ground beside the trail is not easy for her.

DAY THREE–DAY FIVE

Mile after plodding mile, the days go by. In the caravan they talk about MEGIDDO, 10 miles west, where Solomon kept his stables for 900 chariots and horses. Here, it is said, the last battle for human salvation will be waged.
(Armageddon = Har-Megiddo = mountain of Megiddo)

DAY SIX

The caravan climbs into the mountains. In the village of NAIN, famed for its flowers and climate, Jesus will restore a widow's son to life.

DAY SEVEN

The Sabbath observed. No traveling this day.

DAY EIGHT

Climbing still. Slow going, yet Joseph and Mary are excited by being for the first time in the places they've learned about in synagogue. There's MOUNT GILBOA! Where Saul and Jonathan were slain by the Philistines and David lamented the loss of his beloved friend: "No dew nor rain nor fields of corn let there ever be upon you . . .'

DAY NINE

The central market of DOTHAN. The Torah told how Jacob's son Joseph was sold into slavery by his brothers here. The couple pause to recite a psalm, a special prayer to ward off such trials as Joseph underwent.

DAY TEN–DAY THIRTEEN

Halfway. The SAMARIAN city of SHOMROM–SEBASTE, ancient walled capital of Israel, yet to Joseph a desecrated city, its buildings more Greek than Jewish, and filled with foreigners who do not believe in God. Three days here outside the walls. Joseph is anxious to push on but this is a trading center and the caravan merchants are too busy to leave.

Ten miles southwest is SHECHEM, noted for the wealth and arrogance of its citizens who are not Jews, but Samaritans. Mary yearns, as do all Jews, for a cup of curative water from JACOB'S WELL, but it is forbidden territory and leaving the caravan might mean being killed by the Samaritans. At Jacob's Well Jesus will meet a Samaritan woman and promise her eternal life.

DAY FOURTEEN

The Sabbath observed. No traveling. Mary needs the rest. Joseph is worried for her.

DAY SEVENTEEN

The small wayside station of RAMALLAH. Here, at last, the first glimpse of the holy city of JERUSALEM, its golden pinnacles glittering in the sun, 10 miles distant. With a full view of the land below, the travelers pray David's psalm, "If I forget thee, O Jerusalem..."

DAY EIGHTEEN

JERUSALEM. Crowded, filled with Roman soldiers. Arrival at the home of Mary's first cousin, Elisabeth, and her husband the priest Zacharias, whose six-month-old baby will be known as John the Baptist. The two couples meet in awe. They are the only people in the world who know the world's most tremendous news, and yet they can say nothing.

DAY NINETEEN

Joseph busies himself about Jerusalem securing exit visas. He gawks at the paved streets, the covered shops, the Roman barracks, at the five great palaces and the huge Roman fortress named for Mark Antony—and especially at the great Temple, its eaves and pinnacles sheathed in pure gold. Mary is puzzled—and not for the first time—by the ways of God. Her time is near. Would it not be fitting that her holy Baby be born in that holy temple? But at dawn they must leave...

DAY FIFTEEN

Joseph and Mary travel around the new city of SHILOH, and mourn for the old SHILOH, a sad and lonely vista of broken-down buildings and shattered altars. Once it possessed the now-lost ARK OF THE COVENANT, the revered sign of God's presence. Mary trembles at the thought that she is carrying the Saviour of her people, a *living* Ark!

DAY SIXTEEN

BETHEL. As devout Jews, Joseph and Mary pause for special prayers where Abraham offered his sacrifices to God, and Jacob dreamed of angels climbing up and down a ladder to Heaven.

DAY TWENTY

Late this day the weary couple pass through the walls of BETHLEHEM, a center for sheep and cattle farming, known for the sweet water of its wells, its synagogue, for King David's house and land.

Joseph is alarmed. Mary's birthing pains have begun. But first he rushes to register with the Romans before it is too late. Then he seeks lodging. But the town is swarming with other members of David's tribe and nothing is available. Frantically, they leave the town and find shelter in one of the caves that shepherds use for stables. There are hayracks and mangers there, and a warming fire.

On this night, Mary's Child, the Son of God, is born. The journey is ended ... and begun.

COME, ALL YE FAITHFUL

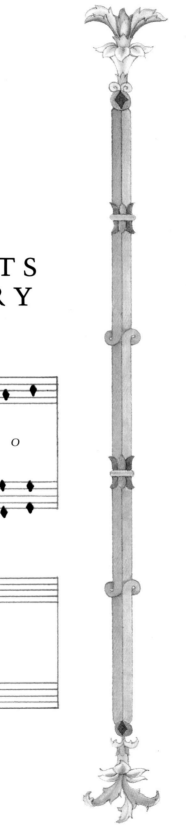

CHAPTER

II

PREPARING OUR HEARTS
IN PRAYER AND POETRY

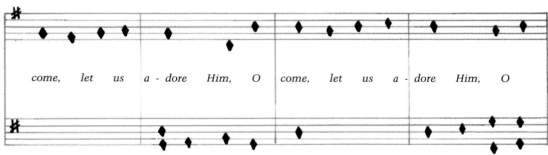

come, let us a-dore Him, O come, let us a-dore Him, O

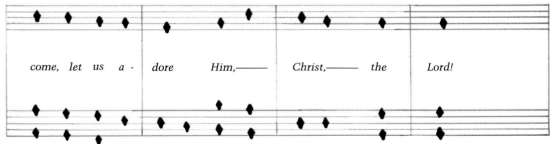

come, let us a-dore Him,——— Christ,——— the Lord!

THE CHRISTMAS STORY

And there were in the same country shepherds abiding in the field, keeping watch over their flock by night. And, lo, the angel of the Lord came upon them, and the glory of the Lord shone round about them: and they were sore afraid. And the angel said unto them, Fear not: for, behold, I bring you good tidings of great joy, which shall be to all people. For unto you is born this day in the city of David a Savior, which is Christ the Lord. And this shall be a sign unto you; Ye shall find the babe wrapped in swaddling clothes, lying in a manger. And suddenly there was with the angel a multitude of the heavenly host praising God, and saying,

Glory to God in the highest,
and on earth peace,
good will toward men.

(Luke 2:8-14)

FROM LET US KEEP CHRISTMAS

Whatever else be lost among the years,
Let us keep Christmas still a shining thing:
Whatever doubts assail us, or what fears,
Let us hold close one day, remembering
Its poignant meaning for the hearts of men.
Let us get back our childlike faith again.

Grace Noll Crowell

A TIME LIKE THIS

It was a time like this
war and tumult of war,
a horror in the air.
Hungry yawned the abyss—
and yet there came the star
and the child most wonderfully there.

It was a time like this
of fear & lust for power,
license & greed & blight—
and yet the Prince of bliss
came in the darkest hour
in quiet & silent light.

And in a time like this
how celebrate his birth
when all things fall apart?
Ah! wonderful it is
with no room on the earth
the stable is our heart.

Madeleine L'Engle

CHRISTMAS DAYBREAK

Before the paling of the stars,
Before the winter morn,
Before the earliest cockcrow,
Jesus Christ was born:
Born in a stable,
Cradled in a manger,
In the world His hands had made,
Born a stranger.

Priest and king lay fast asleep
In Jerusalem,
Young and old lay fast asleep
In crowded Bethlehem:
Saint and angel, ox and ass,
Kept a watch together,
Before the Christmas daybreak
In the winter weather.

Jesus on His Mother's breast
In the stable cold,
Spotless Lamb of God was He,
Shepherd of the fold.
Let us kneel with Mary Maid,
With Joseph bent and hoary,
With saint and angel, ox and ass,
To hail the King of Glory.

Christina Georgina Rossetti

THE BLESSING
OF THE CRÈCHE

Sue Monk Kidd

One Christmas I traveled to Bethlehem. There is a little shop there that sits on a winding road, not far from the nativity cave. As I stepped inside, a dark-eyed man with a wide, white smile appeared at my elbow. "May I help you, Madam?" he said.

"I'm looking for a crèche," I replied. "A nativity set."

His eyes gleamed like two black pearls. He made a little bow to the rear of the store. I followed him along an aisle until suddenly he stepped aside, sweeping out his arm, and there in the middle of a table sat a crèche. A crèche so splendid it seemed to glow with the ancient holiness that inspired it. It had been carved from the olive trees that dotted the Judean hills like green umbrellas. The rich wood shone warm and golden in the dim light of the little shop. I touched each piece with reverence. Only moments before I had stood in the heart of the holy cave where Jesus was born, and my heart was still full.

The salesman stood nearby. "You like, Madam?" he asked, as my fingers touched the tiny tips of the star carved atop the stable.

He stepped closer. "It is the finest wood. And the workmanship is unmatched," he said. I nodded.

I walked around the table, trying to make up my mind. "I'm not sure," I said.

"Ah, but Madam, you must have it!" he said. "A Bethlehem crèche has secret blessings!"

In the end I purchased the crèche, not for its alleged "secret blessings," but because of its irresistible beauty and because I was in Bethlehem and the long-ago miracle still lived in the air.

I stored it in a cardboard box in the attic. The next Christmas, I wanted to make the crèche's first appearance beneath our tree special. I thought and wondered. How could it touch my family with the Bethlehem miracle? I found myself remembering the words of the salesman, "A Bethlehem crèche has secret blessings." Perhaps he was right. Perhaps God *could* bless and inspire our lives through its presence, if only we let Him. And not just with a Bethlehem

crèche . . . but *any* crèche, even the tiny one my daughter had made from popsicle sticks one Christmas past.

So I sat down and wrote a prayer. Then, filled with anticipation, I climbed to the attic and brought down the cardboard box. That night, with the tree lights shining in the darkness and dancing on the windows, my family gathered around the tree. An almost reverent silence settled about us as softly as a whisper in church. My husband opened the lid. The children took turns standing each item of the crèche beneath the tree as I read my prayer aloud:

It is time, Lord. Time to take the holy drama from this cardboard box and set it beneath the tree. As I blow away the dust, may this little crèche come to life in our home and bestow its secret blessings.
Bless this wooden stable, Lord. This lowly abode of cows and donkeys. May it keep me humble this Christmas.
Bless this tiny star beaming at the top. May it light my eyes with the wonder of Your caring.
Bless the little angel. May her song flow through our house and fill it with smiles.
Bless this caring shepherd and the small lamb cradled in his arms. May it whisper of Your caring embrace on my life.
Bless these Wise Men bearing splendid gifts. May they inspire me to lay my shining best at Your feet.
Bless this earthly father in his simple robe. May he remind me of all You have entrusted to my care.
Bless this Virgin Mother. May she teach me patience as I tend to my own little ones.
And bless this Baby nestled in the hay. May the love He brought to earth that Bethlehem night so fill my heart with compassion and warmth that it becomes a Christmas gift to others.
Now the crèche is here, Lord . . . and we are holy participants. May Your secret blessings come to us as a spark from Your glory . . . a candle that never goes out. Amen

I can't tell you *exactly* what happened to us that night, but I do know that I experienced a special holiness and a reverence for our family that stayed with me all through the Christmas season. That was my "secret blessing," and perhaps each of us shared the same "secret." For this little ritual has become the single most important Christmas preparation for our family.

LONG, LONG AGO

Winds through the olive trees
Softly did blow,
Round little Bethlehem
Long, long ago.

Sheep on the hillside lay
Whiter than snow;
Shepherds were watching them
Long, long ago.

Then from the happy sky
Angels bent low,
Singing their songs of joy
Long, long ago.

For in a manger bed,
Cradled we know,
Christ came to Bethlehem
Long, long ago.

Katherine Parker

For God so loved the world,
that he gave his only begotten
Son, that whosoever believeth
in him should not perish, but
have everlasting life.

John 3:16

We hear the Christmas angels
The great glad tidings tell;
O come to us, abide with us,
Our Lord Immanuel!

Hymn

Make me pure, Lord; Thou art holy;
Make me meek, Lord; Thou wert lowly;
Now beginning, and alway:
Now begin, on Christmas day.

Gerard Manley Hopkins

THE LIGHT OF BETHLEHEM'S STAR

It was Sunday before Christmas and I arrived early to church. From a front pew I had a good view of the life-size Nativity scene. As I focused on the kneeling shepherds, I was struck by the awe and reverence carved into the faces of these wooden statues. Suddenly I seemed to be with the real shepherds, spun back two thousand years in an instant, as though time had never been.

How had I missed it before? For weeks I had been looking at this same scene from the back of the church while my mind thought of gift buying, planning a party, sending cards. The eyes of my spirit had been blinded. But now, for one intense moment, I saw what the shepherds saw—the Christ.

As I knelt there, I began to see a little, perhaps, of what God sees. The essence of things so often missed or taken for granted—the true beauty of relationships with friends and family, the blessing of good health, the joy of being alive. And suddenly, for me, it *was* Christmas.

Perhaps if we would take a closer look at *each day*, allow the light of Bethlehem's Star to illuminate every moment, we would be able to enjoy the true beauty of the world around us—on Christmas and every day!

Doris Haase

A PLACE OF SAFETY

At Christmastime, I like to think of Jesus being born anew in my heart. The time I sense it best is after all the rush of card writing, shopping, wrapping, decorating, and baking is done and I'm sitting in the darkened church with my spiritual family, holding my little lighted candle, and the first soft strains of "Silent Night" begin. My faith is freshened and renewed and, yes, reborn. But I know that, like Mary's Baby, this new little child of the Spirit needs a safe place in which to grow. My renewed faith must be protected from Herod (all those things that try to distract me from God). This means finding my own quiet refuge, a place where I can go to pray, away from all the commotion and clamor of daily living. Usually, my sanctuary is the spare bedroom, but if it's occupied, I can always find another Egypt, whether it's in the storage room, laundry, or even the bathroom. If none of those places is available, there's always my car! The important thing is that I find a private place apart, where the fragile new rebirth of faith can be nurtured every day and from which it can emerge to do its work in the world.

Perhaps during this holy season, as Christ is reborn in your heart, you'll want to prepare a safe place for the Baby to grow, even after the crèche has been put away—a quiet place where you can be alone to pray. If you go there every day, you may soon find that the *real* sanctuary you have built is an inner one, a window into wonder that can never be taken away.

Marilyn Morgan Helleberg

CHRISTMAS HUSH

May the quietness of Christmas,
The calm and holy hush
Of that first advent season,
Still our Christmas rush.

May our memories of the manger
Reassure us, ease the stress
Of troubled hearts in troubled times
With His peace and quietness.

Kay L. Halliwill

MAY YOU HAVE JOY

May you have joy in the mad rush of preparation;
May you know peace in the tiny margins of time
around the busy days;
May you have star-shine in clear night skies
for looking at;
May you have silence now and then; and
above all—beyond all else—
May you have love to give and to receive.

Elizabeth Searle Lamb

CHRISTMAS BELLS

I heard the bells on Christmas Day
Their old, familiar carols play,
And wild and sweet
The words repeat
Of peace on earth, good-will to men!

Henry Wadsworth Longfellow

A CHRISTMAS SONG

Everywhere, everywhere, Christmas to-night!
Christmas in lands of fir tree and pine;
Christmas in lands of palm tree and vine;
Christmas where snow peaks stand solemn and
    white;
Christmas where cornfields lie sunny and bright:
Everywhere, everywhere, Christmas to-night!

Phillips Brooks

FOR THEM

Before you bid, for Christmas' sake,
Your guests to sit at meat,
Oh please to save a little cake
For them that have no treat.

Before you go down party-dressed
In silver gown or gold,
Oh please to send a little vest
To them that still go cold.

Before you give your girl and boy
Gay gifts to be undone,
Oh please to spare a little toy
To them that will have none.

Before you gather round the tree
To dance the day about,
Oh please to give a little glee
To them that go without.

Eleanor Farjeon

THE JOY OF GIVING

Somehow, not only for Christmas
But all the long year through,
The joy that you give to others
Is the joy that comes back to you;
And the more you spend in blessing
The poor and lonely and sad,
The more of your heart's possessing
Returns to make you glad.

John Greenleaf Whittier

For who hath nought to give but love,
Gives all his heart away,
And giving all, hath all to give,
Another Christmas Day.

Charles W. Kennedy

Oh Lord, this is a season of light,
of Bethlehem candles burning.
Help me to bask in that light
and in that full radiance
see my brother as he really is.

Help me to sustain that
recognition of him
As the seasons turn
and the night sky, once more,
Is aburst with the
brilliance of Your birth.

Amen

Van Varner

41

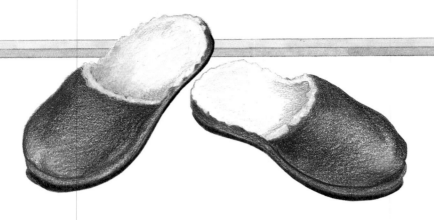

PASSING THE FLAME OF THE CHRIST CANDLE

A group of us were caroling at the convalescent home where a frail gentleman was seated in a wheelchair in front of me. He wore a bulky gray sweater that made him look like a giraffe in elephant's clothing. His mouth gaped in a smile until a nurse unknowingly knocked off one of his navy-blue slippers. She was gone before he could protest. As we sang, his black-stocking foot fished unsuccessfully on the floor for his slipper. Minutes passed. His foot kept moving. Then blushing, I stepped forward, knelt beside him, and pulled the slipper onto his foot. I thought of Jesus washing the disciples' feet saying "I have not come to be served but to serve" (Matthew 20:28, RSV). When I looked up, the man's grateful eyes met mine, and something passed between us. I think it was the flame of the Christ candle.

It seems that the flame can be passed quite simply . . . by washing a foot or slipping on a shoe. Perhaps, as Mother Teresa says, "It is not how much we do, but how much love we put into the doing."

Terry Helwig

THIS DAY

This Day won't come my way again,
So let me take the time,
To make another's holiday
As full of joy as mine.

This Day won't come my way again,
So let me freely share,
The blessings of the Season
With those for whom I care.

This Day won't come my way again,
So let me spread His love.
As God did when He sent His Son,
Christ Jesus from above.

                    Rosalyn Hart Finch

JOY TO THE WORLD!

CHAPTER

III

CLASSIC
CHRISTMAS STORIES

"CHRISTMAS EVE"

from

THE TWENTY-FOUR DAYS
BEFORE CHRISTMAS

Madeleine L'Engle

When we woke up on Christmas Eve morning, we ran to the windows. Not only was the ground white, but we couldn't even see the road. Mother said the snow plow went through at five o'clock so the farmers could get the milk out, and Daddy had followed the milk trucks, but the road had already filled in again.

We ate breakfast quickly, put on snow suits, and ran out to play. The snow was soft and sticky, the very best kind for making snowmen and building forts. We spent the morning making a Christmas snowman, and started a fort around him. John is good at cutting blocks out of snow like an Eskimo. We weren't nearly finished, though, when Mother called us in for lunch.

After lunch Suzy said, "I might as well go upstairs and have my nap and get it over with." We have to have naps on Christmas Eve if we want to stay after the Pageant for the Christmas Eve service. Suzy is very business-like about things like naps. Mother looked a little peculiar, but she didn't say anything, and Suzy went upstairs to bed, taking a book. She can't read, but she likes looking at pictures. Mother lit the kitchen fire and sat in front of it to read to John and me. We were just settled and comfortable when the phone rang. Mother answered it. We listened.

"Yes, I was afraid of that . . . Of course . . . They'll be disappointed, but they'll have to understand." She hung up and turned to John and me.

"What's the matter?" John asked.

Mother said, "The Pageant's been called off because of the blizzard, and so has the Christmas Eve service."

"But *why*?" John demanded.

Mother looked out the windows. "How do you think anybody could travel in this weather, John? We're completely snowed in. The road men are concentrating on keeping the main roads open, but all the side roads are unusable. That means that about three quarters of the village is snowed in just like us. I'm sorry about the angel, Vicky. I know it's a big disappointment to you, but remember that lots of other children are disappointed, too."

I looked over at the crèche, with Mary and Joseph now in their places, and the manger still empty and waiting for the baby Jesus. "Well, I guess lots worse things could happen." I thought—If this means Mother will be home for Christmas...

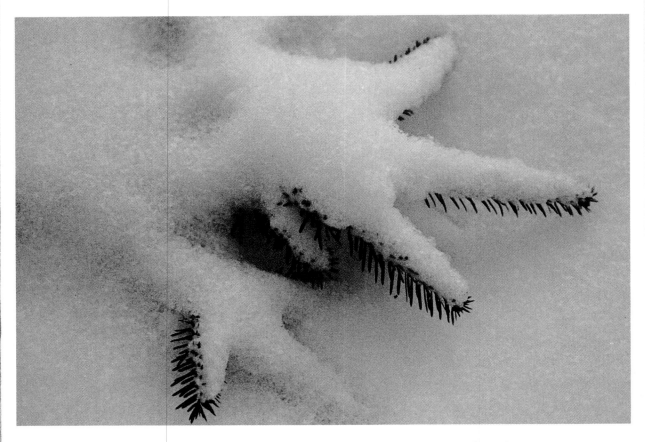

And then I thought—Blizzards can stop pageants, but they can't stop babies, and if the baby starts coming she'll have to go to the hospital anyhow...

"You're a good girl to be so philosophical," Mother said.

But I didn't really think I was being philosophical.

John said, "Anyhow, it looks as though the baby's going to wait till after Christmas."

Mother answered, "Let's hope so."

was lying in the big bed and smiling. In the crook of her arm was a little bundle. We tiptoed closer. The bundle was our baby brother. His face was all puckered and rosy. His eyes were closed tight. He had a wisp of dampish hair. He had a tiny bud of a mouth. One little fist was close to his cheek. We stood and stared at him. We were too excited and awed to speak.

Mother asked, "Isn't he beautiful?" and we all nodded.

Then Daddy shooed us out. "All right. Time for bed, everybody."

John went off to his room, and Suzy and I to ours. When we had undressed and brushed our teeth and Suzy was in bed, I stood at the window. The snow had stopped. The ground was a great soft blanket of white, broken by the dark lines of trees and the gay colors of the outdoor tree. The sky was dark and clear and crusted with stars. I watched and watched, and there was one star that was brighter and more sparkling than any of the others.

The Christmas star.

Mother was home. Daddy was home. Our baby brother was home. We were all together.

I whispered, "Thank you."

And the light shone right into my heart.

THE OTHER WISE MAN

Henry Van Dyke

In the days when Augustus Caesar was master of many kings and Herod reigned in Jerusalem, there lived in the city of Ecbatana, in the mountains of Persia, a certain Artaban, the Median. From the roof of his house he could look over the rising battlements of the seven walls encircling the royal treasury, to the hill where the summer palace of the Parthian emperors glittered like a jewel in a crown.

Around the dwelling of Artaban spread a fair garden, a tangle of flowers and fruit trees, watered by streams descending from the slopes of Mount Orontes, and made musical by innumerable birds. But in the soft, odorous darkness of the late September night, all sounds were hushed save the splashing of water. High above the trees a dim glow of light shone through the curtained arches of the upper chamber, where the master of the house was holding council with his friends.

He was a tall, dark man of about 40 years, with brilliant eyes set near together under his broad brow, and firm lines graven around his fine, thin lips; the brow of a dreamer and the mouth of a soldier, a man of sensitive feeling but inflexible will—one of those born for a life of quest. His robe was of pure white wool, thrown over a tunic of silk; and a white, pointed cap rested on his flowing black hair. It was the dress of the ancient priesthood of the Magi, called the fire worshipers.

"Welcome!" he said, in his low, pleasant voice, as one after another entered the room. "You are all welcome, and this house grows bright with the joy of your presence."

There were nine men, differing in age, but alike in the richness of their dress of many-colored silks, in the massive golden collars around their necks marking them as Parthian nobles, and in the winged circles of gold resting upon their breasts, the sign of the followers of Zoroaster. They took their places around a black altar where a tiny flame burned. Artaban, standing beside it, and waving a barsom of thin tamarisk branches above the fire, fed it with dry sticks of pine and fragrant oils. Then he began the ancient chant, and the voices of his companions joined in the beautiful hymn to Ahura Mazda:

"We worship the Spirit Divine,
All wisdom and goodness possessing..."

The fire rose with the chant, throbbing as if made of musical flame, until it illuminated the whole apartment. The floor was laid with tiles of dark blue veined with white. Pilasters of twisted silver stood out against the blue walls; the clerestory of round-arched windows above was hung with azure silk. The vaulted ceiling was a pavement of sapphires, like the body of heaven in its clearness, sown with silver stars. In effect the room was like a quiet, starry night, flushed in the east with rosy promise of the dawn. As the house of a man should, it expressed the character and spirit of the master.

When the song ended, Artaban invited his friends to be seated, and said: "You have come tonight at my call, as faithful scholars of Zoroaster, to renew your faith in the God of Purity, even as this fire has been rekindled on the altar. We worship not the fire, but him of whom it is the chosen symbol, because it is the purest of all created things. It speaks to us of one who is Light and Truth. Is it not so, my father?"

"It is well said, my son," answered the venerable Abgarus. "The enlightened are never idolaters: they lift the veil of form and go into the shrine of reality."

"Hear me, then, my father and my friends," said Artaban. "We have searched the secrets of nature together, and studied the healing virtues of water and fire and the plants. We have read also the books of prophecy in which the future is dimly foretold. But the highest of all learning is the knowledge of the stars. To trace their courses is to untangle the threads of the mystery of life from beginning to end. But is not our knowledge of them still incomplete? Are there not many stars still beyond our horizon—lights known only to the dwellers in the far southland, among the spice trees of Punt and the gold mines of Ophir?"

There was a murmur of assent.

"The stars," said Tigranes, "are the thoughts of the Eternal. They are numberless. The wisdom of the Magi is the greatest of all wisdoms on earth, because it knows its own ignorance. And that is the secret of power. We keep men always looking for a new sunrise. But we ourselves know that the darkness is equal to the light, that the conflict between them will never be ended."

"That does not satisfy me," answered Artaban. "For, if the waiting must be endless and unfulfilled, then it would not be wisdom to look and wait. The new sunrise will certainly dawn in the appointed time. Do not our own books tell us that men will see the brightness of a great light?"

"That is true," said Abgarus. "Every faithful disciple of Zoroaster knows the prophecy: 'In that day Sosiosh the Victorious shall arise out of the prophets. Around him shall shine a mighty brightness; he shall make life everlasting, incorruptible, and immortal, and the dead shall rise again.' "

"My father," said Artaban with a glow on his face, "I have carried this prophecy in the secret place of my soul. Religion without a great hope would be like an altar without a living fire. And I have read other words which speak yet more clearly of this." He drew from his tunic two small rolls of fine linen with writing upon them. "Long before our fathers came into the land of Babylon, there were wise men in Chaldea, from whom the first of the Magi learned the secret of the heavens. And of these Balaam was one of the mightiest. Hear the words of his prophecy: "There shall come a Star out of Jacob; and a Scepter shall rise out of Israel.' "

"Judah was a captive by the waters of Babylon," said

Tigranes with contempt, "and the sons of Jacob were in bondage to our kings. The tribes of Israel are scattered through the mountains like lost sheep. From the remnant that swells in Judea under the yoke of Rome neither star nor scepter shall arise."

"And yet," answered Artaban, "it was the Hebrew Daniel who was most honored of our great King Cyrus. A sure prophet and a reader of the thoughts of God, Daniel proved himself to our people. And he wrote: 'Know therefore and understand, that from the going forth of the commandment to restore and to build Jerusalem unto the Messiah the Prince shall be seven weeks, and threescore and two weeks.'"

"But, my son," said Abgarus, "these are mystical numbers. Who can unlock their meaning?"

Artaban answered: "My three companions among the Magi—Caspar, Melchior, Balthazar—and I have searched the ancient tablets of Chaldea and computed the time. It falls in this year. We have studied the sky, and in the spring of the year we saw two of the greatest stars draw near together in the sign of the Fish, which is the house of the Hebrews. We also saw a new star there, which shone for one night and vanished. Now again the two great planets are meeting. This night is their conjunction. My three brothers are watching at the ancient Temple of the Seven Spheres, at Borsippa, in Babylonia, and I am watching here. If the star shines again, in ten days we will set out together for Jerusalem, to see and worship the promised one who shall be born King of Israel. I believe the sign will come. I have made ready for the journey. I have sold my house and my possessions, and bought these jewels—a sapphire, a ruby, and a pearl—to carry as tribute to the King. And I ask you to go with me on the pilgrimage that we may together find the Prince."

From the inmost fold of his girdle he drew out three great

gems—one blue as a fragment of the night sky, one redder than a ray of sunrise, one pure as the peak of a snow mountain at twilight.

But a veil of doubt and mistrust came over his friends' faces, like a fog creeping up from the marshes to hide the hills.

"Artaban, this is a vain dream," Tigranes said. "It comes from too much looking upon the stars and the cherishing of lofty thoughts. No king will ever rise from the broken race of Israel, and no end will ever come to the eternal strife of light and darkness. He who looks for it is a chaser of shadows. Farewell."

Each of the others in turn said the quest was not for him. But Abgarus, the oldest, who lingered after the others had gone, said gravely: "My son, it may be that the light of truth is in this sign that has appeared in the skies; or it may be that it is only a shadow of the light, as Tigranes has said. But better to follow even the shadow of the best than to remain content with the worst. And those who would see wonderful things must often be ready to travel alone. I am too old for this journey, but my heart shall be a companion of the pilgrimage. Go in peace."

So, Artaban was left in solitude. For a long time he watched the flame that flickered upon the altar. Then he walked to the roof terrace. The cool wind that heralds daybreak was drawing downward from Mount Orontes. Birds, half awakened, chirped among the rustling leaves, and the smell of ripened grapes came in brief wafts from the arbors.

Far over the eastern plain a white mist stretched like a lake. But where the distant peaks of Zagros serrated the western horizon, the sky was clear. Jupiter and Saturn rolled together like drops of lambent flame about to blend into one.

As Artaban watched them, behold, an azure spark was born out of the darkness beneath, rounding itself with purple splendors to a crimson sphere, then spiring upward through rays of saffron and orange into a point of white radiance. Tiny and infinitely remote, yet perfect in every part, it pulsated as if the Magian's own three jewels had mingled and been transformed into a living heart of light.

He bowed his head. "It is the sign," he said. "The King is coming, and I will go to meet him."

By the Waters of Babylon

All night long Vasda, the swiftest of Artaban's horses, had been waiting, saddled and bridled, in her stall, pawing the ground impatiently and shaking her bit. Before the birds had fully roused to their high, joyful chant of morning song, before the mist had begun to lift lazily from the plain, the Other Wise Man was in the saddle, riding swiftly westward.

How close, how intimate is the comradeship between a man and his favorite horse on a long journey. They drink at the same spring, sleep under the same guardian stars. The master shares his meal with his hungry companion, and feels the soft lips caressing his palm as they close over the morsel of bread. In the gray dawn he is roused by the gentle stir of a warm breath over his sleeping face, and looks up into the eyes of his faithful fellow traveler, ready for the toil of the day. And then, through the keen morning air, the swift hoofs beat their spirited music along the road, keeping time to the pulsing of two hearts.

Artaban must indeed ride wisely and well to keep the appointed hour with the other Magi; for the route was 150 parasangs, and 15 was the utmost he could travel in a day. But he pushed forward, making the fixed distance every day, though he must travel late into the night, and in the morning long before sunrise.

He passed along the brown slopes of Mount Orontes, furrowed by the rocky courses of a hundred torrents.

He crossed the level plains of the Nisacans, where the famous herds of horses tossed their heads at Vasda's approach,

and galloped away with a thunder of many hoofs.

He traversed the fertile fields of Concabar, where the dust from the threshing floors filled the air with a golden mist, half hiding the huge temple of Astarte with its 400 pillars.

At Baghistan, among the rich gardens watered by fountains from the rock, he looked up at the mountain thrusting its immense rugged brow out over the road, and saw the figure of King Darius trampling upon his fallen foe, and the proud list of his conquests graven high on the face of the eternal cliff.

Over many a cold and desolate pass, crawling painfully across the windswept shoulders of the hills; down many a black mountain gorge, where the river roared and raced before him like a savage guide; through the oak groves of Carine and the dark Gates of Zagros, walled in by precipices; over the broad rice fields where autumnal vapors spread their deathly mists; following the river Gyndes, under tremulous shadows of poplar and tamarind; and out upon the flat plain, where the road ran straight as an arrow through the stubble fields and parched meadows; across the swirling floods of Tigris and the many channels of Euphrates—Artaban pressed onward until he arrived, at nightfall on the tenth day, beneath the shattered walls of populous Babylon.

He would gladly have turned into the city to find rest and refreshment for himself and Vasda. But it was three hours' journey yet to the Temple of the Seven Spheres, and he must reach the place by midnight if he would find his comrades waiting. So he rode steadily on.

A grove of date palms made an island of gloom in the pale-yellow sea of stubble fields. The grove was close and silent as the tomb. Scenting some danger, Vasda picked her way delicately, carrying her head low. At last she gave a quick breath of anxiety, and stood stock-still, quivering in every muscle, before a dark object in the shadow of the last palm tree.

Artaban dismounted. The dim starlight revealed the form of a man lying across the road, one of the poor Hebrew exiles who still dwelt in great numbers in the vicinity. His skin, dry and yellow as parchment, bore the mark of the deadly fever which ravaged the marshlands in autumn. The chill of death was in his lean hand, and when released the arm fell back inertly.

Artaban turned away with a thought of pity, consigning the body to that burial the Magians deemed most fitting—the

funeral of the desert, from which the kites and vultures rise
on dark wings, and the beasts of prey slink furtively away,
leaving only white bones in the sand. But, as he turned, a
ghostly sigh came from the man's lips. The bony fingers
closed convulsively on the Magian's robe and held him fast.

Artaban's spirit throbbed with a dumb resentment. What
claim had this unknown fragment of human life upon his
compassion or his service? If he lingered but for an hour he
could hardly reach Borsippa at the appointed time; his
companions would go without him. Should he turn aside from
the following of the star, risk the great reward of his divine
faith, to give a cup of cold water to a poor, perishing Hebrew?

"God of Truth and Purity," he prayed, "direct me in the
holy path, the way of wisdom which thou only knowest."

Then Artaban turned back to the sick man. Carrying him
to the foot of the palm tree, he brought water and moistened
the sufferer's brow and mouth. He mingled a draught of one of
those simple but potent remedies he carried always in his
girdle—for the Magians were skillful physicians as well as
astrologers—and poured it slowly between the colorless lips.
Hour after hour he labored, and at last the man's strength
returned. He sat up and looked about him.

"Who art thou?" he said.

"I am Artaban the Magian, and I am going to Jerusalem in search of one who is to be born a great Prince and Deliverer of all men. I dare not delay any longer. But see, here is all I have left of bread and wine, and a potion of healing herbs."

The Jew raised his trembling hand solemnly to heaven. "May the God of Abraham and Isaac and Jacob bless and prosper the journey of the merciful. I have nothing to give thee in return—only this: that our prophets have said the Messiah should be born not in Jerusalem, but in Bethlehem of Judah. May the Lord bring thee in peace and safety to that place."

It was already long past midnight. Artaban rode in haste, and Vasda fled over the ground like a gazelle. But the first beam of the sun sent her shadow before her as she entered upon the final stadium of the journey, and Artaban, anxiously scanning the great mound of Nimrod and the Temple of the Seven Spheres, could discern no trace of his friends.

Artaban dismounted and climbed to the highest terrace, looking toward the west. The huge desolation of the marshes stretched away to the horizon and the border of the desert, but there was no sign of the caravan of the Wise Men, far or near.

At the terrace edge he saw a cairn of broken bricks, and under them a piece of parchment. He read: "We can delay no longer. We go to find the King. Follow us across the desert."

Artaban sat down and covered his head in despair. "How can I cross the desert," said he, "with no food and with a spent horse? I must return to Babylon, sell my sapphire and buy a train of camels, and provision for the journey. Only God the merciful knows whether I shall not lose the sight of the King because I tarried to show mercy."

For the Sake of a Little Child

There was a silence in the Hall of Dreams. And through this silence I saw, but very dimly, the Other Wise Man's figure passing over the dreary undulations of the desert, high upon the back of his camel, rocking steadily onward like a ship over the waves.

The land of death spread its cruel net around him. The stony wastes bore no fruit but briers and thorns. Arid and inhospitable mountain ranges rose before him. Shifting hills of treacherous sand were heaped like tombs along the horizon. By day the fierce heat pressed its intolerable burden on the quivering air; and no living creature moved but tiny jerboas scuttling through the parched bushes, or lizards vanishing in the clefts of the rock. By night jackals barked in the distance, while a blighting chill followed the fever of the day. Through heat and cold, the Magian moved on.

Then I saw the gardens and orchards of Damascus, watered by the streams of Abana and Pharpar. I saw the long, snowy ridge of Hermon, the dark groves of cedars, the valley of the Jordan, the blue waters of the Lake of Galilee, and, far beyond, the highlands of Judah. Through all these Artaban moved steadily onward until he arrived at Bethlehem, bearing his ruby and his pearl to offer to the King. "For now at last," he said, "I shall surely find him, though it be alone and later than my brethren."

The streets of the village seemed deserted. From the open door of a low stone cottage Artaban heard the sound of a woman's voice singing softly. He entered and found a young mother hushing her baby to rest. She told him of the strangers from the far east who had appeared in the village three days ago. They said that a star had guided them to the place where Joseph of Nazareth was lodging with his wife Mary and her newborn child Jesus, and how they had paid reverence to the child, and laid gifts of gold and frankincense and myrrh at his feet.

"But the travelers disappeared again, as suddenly as they had come. We were afraid at the strangeness of their visit. The family from Nazareth fled that same night secretly, and it was whispered they were going far away to Egypt. Ever since, something evil hangs over the village. They say Roman soldiers are coming from Jerusalem to force a new tax from us, and the men have hidden themselves to escape it."

The child in her arms looked up in Artaban's face and smiled, stretching out its rosy hands to him. His heart warmed to the touch. "Might not *this* child have been the promised Prince?" he asked himself. "Kings have been born in lowlier houses than this; the favorite of the stars may rise even from a cottage. But no, it has not seemed good to the God of Wisdom to reward my search so easily. The one I seek has gone before me; and now I must follow the King to Egypt."

The young mother laid the babe in its cradle, and set food before the strange guest that fate had brought into her house. It was the plain fare of peasants, but willingly offered, and therefore full of refreshment for the soul as well as for the body. As Artaban ate, the child fell into a happy slumber, and murmured sweetly in its dreams.

But suddenly there came the noise of a wild confusion in the streets, a shrieking and wailing of women's voices, a clangor of trumpets and a desperate cry: "Soldiers! The soldiers of Herod! They are killing our children."

White with terror, the mother crouched motionless in the darkest corner of the room, covering her child with the folds of her robe lest he wake and cry. But Artaban went and stood in the doorway of the house, his broad shoulders filling the portal from side to side.

At the sight of the imposing stranger, the soldiers with bloody hands and dripping swords hesitated. The captain approached to thrust him aside. But Artaban's face was as calm as though he were watching the stars, and in his eyes burned that steady radiance before which even the half-tamed hunting leopard shrinks. He held the soldier silently for an instant, then said in a low voice, "I am alone in this place, and waiting to give this jewel to the prudent captain who will leave me in peace."

He showed the ruby, glistening in his hand like a great drop of blood. The pupils of the captain's eyes expanded with desire, and he stretched out his hand for the ruby.

"March on!" he cried to his men. "There is no child here."

As the clamor and clang of arms passed down the street, Artaban turned his face to the east and prayed: "God of Truth, forgive my sin! I have said the thing that is not, to save the life of a child. And two of my gifts are gone. I have spent for man that which was meant for God. Shall I ever be worthy to see the face of the King?"

But the woman, weeping for joy behind him, said gently, "May the Lord bless thee, and keep thee: the Lord make his face to shine upon thee, and be gracious unto thee: the Lord lift up his countenance upon thee, and give thee peace."

The Way of Sorrow

Then again there was a silence in the Hall of Dreams, and I understood that under the deep, mysterious stillness the years of Artaban were flowing swiftly. I caught only a glimpse, here and there, of him moving among the throngs in populous Egypt, seeking everywhere for signs of the household that had come down from Bethlehem. He found traces under the spreading sycamores of Heliopolis, and beneath the walls of New Babylon beside the Nile—but traces so faint and dim they vanished before him continually, as footprints on the hard river sand glisten for a moment with moisture and then disappear.

I saw him again at the foot of the pyramids, monuments of the perishable glory and imperishable hope of man. He looked up into the vast countenance of the crouching Sphinx, and tried to read the meaning of that inscrutable smile. Was it, indeed, the mockery of all effort and aspiration—the cruel jest of a search that never can succeed? Or was there a touch of encouragement—a promise that even the defeated should attain a victory, the blind see, and the wandering enter the haven at last?

I saw him again in an obscure house of Alexandria, taking counsel with a Hebrew rabbi. The venerable man, bending over the rolls of parchment, read aloud prophecies which foretold the sufferings of the promised Messiah—despised and rejected of men, a man of sorrows.

"And remember, my son," said he, fixing his deep-set eyes upon Artaban, "the King you are seeking is not to be found in a palace, not among the rich and powerful. The light for which the world is waiting is a new light, the glory that shall rise out of patient, triumphant suffering. And the kingdom which is to be established forever is a new kingdom, the royalty of perfect, unconquerable love. I do not know how this shall come to pass, or how the turbulent kings and peoples of earth shall be brought to acknowledge the Messiah. But this I know. Those who seek him will do well to look among the poor and lowly, the sorrowful and oppressed.''

I saw the Other Wise Man traveling and searching among the people of the dispersion, with whom the family from Bethlehem might perhaps have found refuge. He passed through countries where famine lay heavy. He made his dwelling in plague-stricken cities where the sick languished in misery. He visited the oppressed in the gloom of subterranean prisons, the crowded wretchedness of slave markets, the weary toil of galley ships. In all this populous and intricate world of anguish, though he found none to worship, he found many to help. He fed the hungry, healed the sick, and comforted the captive; and his years went by more swiftly than the weaver's shuttle that flashes back and forth through the loom while the invisible pattern is completed.

It seemed almost as if he had forgotten his quest. But once I saw him for a moment as he stood alone at sunrise, waiting at the gate of a Roman prison. He had taken from a secret resting place in his bosom the pearl, the last of his jewels. As he looked at it, a mellower luster, full of shifting gleams of azure and rose, trembled upon its surface. It seemed to have absorbed some reflection of the colors of the lost sapphire and ruby. So the profound, secret purpose of a noble life draws into itself the memories of past joy and past sorrow—all transfused by a subtle magic into its very essence. It becomes more luminous and precious the longer it is carried close to the warmth of the beating heart.

Then, at last, while I was thinking of this pearl, and its meaning, I heard the end of the story of the Other Wise Man.

A Pearl of Great Price

Three-and-thirty years of Artaban's quest had passed, and his hair, once darker than the cliffs of Zagros, was now white as the wintry snow. His eyes, that once flashed like flames of fire, were as embers smoldering among the ashes. Worn and weary and ready to die, but still a pilgrim looking for the King, he had come to Jerusalem. He had often searched the holy city before, without finding any trace of the family who had fled from Bethlehem long ago. But now it seemed as if he must make one more effort.

The children of Israel, scattered in far lands all over the world, had returned to the Temple for the great feast of the Passover. The city was thronged with strangers, and on this day there was a singular agitation. The sky was veiled with a portentous gloom, and currents of excitement seemed to flash through the crowd. The clatter of sandals, and the soft, thick

sound of thousands of bare feet shuffling over the stones, flowed unceasingly along the street leading to the Damascus gate. Seeing a group from his own country, Parthian Jews, Artaban inquired where they were going.

"To the place called Golgotha, outside the city walls," they answered. "Have you not heard? Two famous robbers are to be crucified, and with them a man called Jesus of Nazareth, who has done many wonderful works among the people. But the priests and elders say he must die, because he gave himself

out to be the Son of God. And Pilate has sent him to the cross because he said he was the 'King of the Jews.' "

How strangely these familiar words fell upon the tired heart of Artaban! They had led him for a lifetime over land and sea. Could it be the same at whose birth the star had appeared in heaven, and of whose coming the prophets had spoken? Artaban's heart beat excitedly.

"The ways of God are stranger than the thoughts of men," he said within himself. "It may be that I shall find the King at last, and shall come in time to offer my pearl for his ransom before he dies."

So the old man followed the multitude toward the Damascus gate. Just beyond the entrance of the guardhouse a troop of soldiers came down the street, dragging a young girl with a torn dress. As the Magian paused, she saw his white cap and the winged circle on his breast, and broke from the hands of her tormentors to throw herself at his feet.

"Have pity," she cried, "and save me, for the sake of the God of Purity! My father was a merchant of Parthia, but he is dead, and I am seized for his debts to be sold as a slave. Save me!"

Artaban trembled. It was the old conflict in his soul between faith's expectation and love's impulse. Twice the gift he had consecrated to religion had been drawn from his hand to the service of humanity. This was the third trial, the final choice. Was it his great opportunity or his last temptation? He could not tell. One thing only was sure: to rescue this helpless girl would be a true deed of love. And is not love the light of the soul?

He took the pearl from his bosom. Never had it seemed so luminous, so full of tender, living luster. He laid it in the slave girl's hand. "This is thy ransom, daughter—the last of my treasures I kept for the King."

While he spoke the darkness thickened, and the earth heaved convulsively. House walls rocked, stones crashed into the street, dust clouds filled the air. The soldiers fled in terror. But Artaban and the girl crouched beneath the wall of the Praetorium.

What had he to fear, or to live for? He had parted with the last hope of finding the King. The quest was over and it had failed. But even in that thought, accepted and embraced, there was peace. He knew all was well, because he had done the best that he could from day to day. He had been true to the light given to him. He had looked for more. And if he had not found it, if failure was all, doubtless that was the best that was possible. If he could live his life over again, it could not be otherwise.

One more lingering pulsation of the earthquake, and a heavy tile, shaken from the roof, fell and struck the old man on the temple. He lay with his gray head resting on the girl's shoulder, the blood trickling from the wound. As she bent over him, there came a voice through the twilight like music sounding from a distance.

The old man's lips moved as if in answer, and she heard him say in the Parthian tongue: "Not so, my Lord. For when saw I thee hungry, and fed thee? Or thirsty, and gave thee drink? When saw I thee sick, or in prison, and came unto thee? Three-and-thirty years have I looked for thee; but I have never seen thy face, nor ministered to thee, my King."

He ceased, and the voice came again, very faintly. But now it seemed the maid too understood the words:

"Verily I say unto thee, inasmuch as thou hast done it unto one of the least of these my brethren, thou hast done it unto me."

A calm radiance of wonder and joy lighted the pale face of Artaban like the first ray of dawn. One long, last breath of relief exhaled gently from his lips. His journey was ended. His treasures were accepted. The Other Wise Man had found the King.

THE NIGHT THE STARS SANG

Dorothy Canfield Fisher

At odd, quiet hours in her day, almost every mother wonders about her child's immortal soul. When will it emerge from the little ragamuffin who has just left his wet lollipop on the davenport? When will the person inside come to the surface? Will anyone be there to see, and to wonder?

I know a mother who was there, who did see and who did wonder. She told me about it, and I don't think she will mind if I tell you. It all began a few weeks before Christmas...

"Well," she said cheerily one afternoon to David, her eight-year-old, and two of his friends, "what Christmas songs are you learning in your classroom this year?"

Looking down at his feet, David answered sadly, "Teacher says we can't sing good enough. She's only going to let kids sing in the entertainment who carry a tune."

Inwardly the mother broke into a mother's rage at a teacher. "So that's what she says, does she? What's she for, if not to teach children what they don't know?"

She drew in a deep breath, then said quietly, "Well, how'd you like to practice your song with me?"

Together the four went into the living room to the piano. "What song is your class to sing?"

"It came upon the midnight—" said the three boys, speaking at once.

"That's a nice one," she commented, reaching for the battered songbook on top of the piano. "This is the way it goes." She played the air and sang the first two lines.

They opened their mouths and sang out lustily:

"It came upon the midnight clear

That glorious song of old..."

At the end of that phrase, David's mother stopped abruptly, and for an instant bowed her head over the keys. Her feeling about Teacher made a right-about turn.

She finally lifted her head, turned a smiling face on the three waiting children. "I tell you what," she said, "the way, really, to learn a tune is just one note after another. I'll strike just the two first notes on the piano—It came—" Full of good will the little boys sang with her.

She stopped. Breathed hard.

"Not quite," she said, with a false smile, "Pre-t-ty good. I think we'd better take it one note at a time. Bill, you try it."

After a pause.... "Peter—it's your turn."

That evening, after the children had gone to bed, she told her husband, "You never heard anything like that in your whole life, Harry. Never. You can't imagine what it was like!"

"Oh, yes I can too," he said over his temporarily lowered newspaper. "I've heard plenty of tone-deaf kids hollering. I know what they sound like. There are people, you know, who really can't carry a tune."

Seeing, perhaps, in her face, the mulish mother–stubbornness, he added, with a little exasperation, "What's the use of trying to do what you can't do?"

That was reasonable, she thought. But the next morning,

when she was downtown doing her marketing, she turned in at the public library and picked up two books on teaching music to children.

During the weeks between then and the Christmas entertainment, the mother didn't see how she could ever keep it up. She discovered to her dismay that the little boys had no idea whether a note was higher or lower than the one before it.

She adapted and invented "musical games" to train their ear for this. Standing in a row, their backs to the piano, listening whether the second note was "up hill or down hill" from the first note, the boys thought it as good a game as any other. They laughed raucously over each other's mistakes, ran a contest to see who came out best.

There were times when the mother faltered. Many times. When she saw the ironing heaped high, or when her daughter, Janey, was in bed with a cold, she would say to herself, "Now today I'll just tell the boys that I cannot go on with this. We're not getting anywhere, anyhow."

Then she would remember that Christmas celebrated the birth of the Savior—and that one of Christ's most beloved traits was patience.

So when the boys came storming in, certain that she would not close that door she had half-opened for them, she laid everything aside and went to the piano.

As a matter of fact, they were getting somewhere. Even with their backs to the piano, the boys could now tell, infallibly, whether a second note was above or below the first one. Along about the second week of December, they could all sound—if they remembered to sing softly and to listen to themselves—a note, any note, within their range, she struck on the piano.

After that it went fast; the practicing of the song, repeating it for the at first skeptical and then thoroughly astonished teacher, and then their triumphant report at home, "Teacher says we can sing it good enough. She says we can sing with the others. We practiced going up on the platform this afternoon."

Then the day of the Christmas entertainment: boys clumping up the aisle, the girls switching their short skirts proudly. David's mother clutched her handbag nervously.

The crash from the piano giving them the tone, all the mouths open,

"It came upo-on the midnight clear
That glorious so-ong of old..."

The mother's tense hands relaxed. Teacher's long drill and hers had been successful. It was not howling, it was singing.

There were swelling crescendos and at the lines:
   "The world in so-olemn stillness lay
   To hear the a-angels sing..."
the child voices were hushed in a diminuendo. Part of the
mother's very life, she thought wryly, had been spent in
securing her part of the diminuendo.

So there he stood, her little David, a fully accredited part
of his corner of society, as good as anybody, the threat of the
inferiority feeling averted this time. The door had been
slammed in his face. She had pushed it open, and he had gone
through.

The hymn ended. The burst of parental applause began
clamorously. The third grade filed down from the platform.
Surely, now, the mother thought, David would turn his head
to where she sat and thank her with a look. Just this once.

He did turn his head as he filed by. He looked full at his
family, at his father, his mother, his kid sister, his big brother,
and his sister from the high school. He gave them a formal,
small nod to acknowledge publicly that they were his family.
But his mother knew that his look was not for her alone. It
was just as much for those of his family who had been bored
and impatient spectators of her struggle to help him, as for her
who had given part of her life to roll that stone uphill.

She sighed. Mothers were to accept what they received,
without bitterness, without resentment. After all, that was
what mothers worked for—not for thanks, but to do their job.
The sharp chisel of life, driven home by experience, flaked off
expertly another flint-hard chip from her blithe, selfish
girlhood. It fell away from the woman she was growing to be,
and dropped soundlessly into the abyss of time...

But a few nights later, close to Christmas, the mother

looked out her kitchen window to see if David was returning from a neighbor's. The night was cloudless, cold and still. Her backyard was almost transparent in the pale radiance that fell from the stars.

Then she saw David. Knee-deep in the snow he stood, looking all around him. Then he lifted his face towards the sky. What could he be looking at? Or hearing?

She opened the kitchen door and stepped out into the dark, under the stars. He came quickly to her, and put his arms around her. With every fiber of her body which had borne his, she felt a difference in him.

"It's so still," he said quietly in a hushed voice, a voice she had never heard before.

"All those stars," he murmured dreamily, "they shine so. But they don't make a sound."

He stood a little away from her to look up into her face. "Do you remember—in the song—'the world in solemn stillness lay'?"

The starlight showed him clear, his honest, little-boy eyes wide, fixed trustingly on his mother's, and in them she saw the miracle—the miracle of an awakening soul.

He had not known that he had an inner sanctuary. Now he stood in it, awe-struck at his first sight of beauty, and opened the door to his mother.

As naturally as he breathed, he put into her hands the pure rounded pearl of a shared joy.

"I thought I heard them singing—sort of," he whispered.

"CHRISTMAS"

from

LOVE'S LONG JOURNEY

Janette Oke

One day, as Missie hung the baby's laundry from the lines strung in the one-room house, she suddenly realized to her surprise that only a few days remained until Christmas.

She ducked under a line of hanging diapers and made her way to another homemade calendar clipped on the wall. It was true. There were only four days 'til Christmas.

She looked about her. Christmas? Here? She blinked away tears and scolded herself. But the aching feeling within her was not to be shaken so easily. What could she possibly do to make this shanty ready for Christmas?

That evening as she and Willie sat at their small table to eat their stew and biscuits, Missie brought up the subject.

"Did you realize that in just four days it's Christmas?"

"Christmas?" Willie said, looking surprised. "Christmas already? Boy, how time does fly!"

Missie felt a sharp retort forming on her tongue, but she refused to voice it.

"Christmas!" Willie repeated. "I can hardly believe it."

He finished the biscuit that he was eating. "Guess I can't provide ya with a turkey. Will a roast of venison do?"

"I reckon."

"Be kinda hard havin' Christmas alone, won't it?"

"I've been thinkin' on that," Missie said. "Why don't we have the hands in?"

"In *here*?"

"Why not?"

Willie stared at the lines of hanging baby things. "Not much room."

"I know, but we could make do."

"They could come two at a time, I guess."

"That wouldn't be *Christmas*."

"How'll ya do it, then?"

"I'll set the food out on the table an' the stove an' we'll just help ourselves and sit wherever we fit—on the stools, on the bed—wherever. I think there's one more stool in the bunkhouse—an' Cookie has one in the cookhouse."

Willie laughed. "You've got yer heart set on it, ain't ya?"

Missie lowered her head but made no comment.

"Okay," said Willie, "invite the men."

"Would you invite them, please, Willie? I—I don't see them much."

"Sure, I'll invite 'em. Fer what time?"

"Let's make it one o'clock."

Willie nodded. "An' I'll git ya thet venison roast."

"Could Cookie do the roast in his stove? Then I can have mine free for the other things."

Willie nodded again. "I'll talk to 'im."

Cookie agreed to do the roast, and when the day arrived Missie went to work on the remainder of the meal. She didn't have much to work with, but what she lacked in ingredients, she made up for with ingenuity. She had been hoarding some of her mother's preserves for just such a time as this. She opened them now and used some of the fruit to fill tart shells. She prepared some of the last canned carrots and beans from home to go with the roast venison. The only potatoes left were a few precious ones that she had kept, hoping to plant them in the spring. They looked sorry and neglected, but Missie still prayed that they might have the germ of life left in them. She refused to use any of them now, although the thought of potatoes with the meal made her mouth water. Instead, she baked a big batch of fluffy biscuits and set out her last jar of honey to go with them.

When the men arrived, Cookie proudly carrying his roast of venison, Missie was ready for them.

"Before we eat," Willie said, "I have something else to bring in. We don't have much room, iffen ya noticed"—this brought a guffaw from the men—"so I left it in the other shed."

He soon returned carrying a scrub bush, held upright in a small pail. On its tiny branches hung little bows made from Missie's scraps of yarn.

"Didn't rightly seem like Christmas without a tree," he said apologetically. The men whooped and Missie cried.

When the commotion had died down, Willie moved with difficulty to the middle of the room and led them in prayer:

"Father, we have much to thank You fer. Fer the good-smellin' food of which we are about to partake; fer the warmth of this little room in which we are to share it; fer friends who are here with us an' those who are far away; fer the memories of

other Christmases spent with those we love; fer Nathan Isaiah, our healthy son; and most of all, God, fer my wife who has blessed us all by givin' us this Christmas. We are reminded thet all of these blessin's are extras. Yer special gift to us on this day was Yer Son. We accept thet Gift with our thanks. Amen."

As the menfolk devoured the tasty and plentiful food, Missie sat quietly. She tired to keep her thoughts from wandering to her parents' home. What would it be like if she could be there, right now? In a house big enough to serve a whole family in comfort, with fresh butter, mashed potatoes, turkey, baked squash, and apple pie topped with whipped cream.

She looked at her plate filled with sliced venison and gravy, canned carrots with no garnish, canned yellow beans, and a biscuit with no butter. However, many days during the last year, she had partaken of even simpler fare. She realized that she was eating a rather sumptuous feast, in comparison. The men obviously felt it was such; and when it came time for the tarts and coffee, they licked their lips in anticipation. Missie picked her way across the room to check on Nathan. One could barely move without tripping over feet, but the close proximity just made it easier for laughing together.

"Son," she whispered to the baby, "you're not gonna remember one thing 'bout this, but I want you to get in on it anyway. Your very first Christmas, and I don't even have anything to give you—but a kiss, an' laughter of friends." She took him in her arms.

After the meal, Missie summoned all of her courage and presented each one of the men with a pair of socks and woolen mittens. She was unprepared for their deep appreciation. She realized that for some of them it may have been their first Christmas gift since they were small boys at home.

Cookie shifted his position to "git outta the smoke from the blasted fire—it's a makin' my eyes water."

Clem swallowed over and over, his Adam's apple lurching up and down.

Missie prayed that none of them would feel embarrassed at having nothing to give in return.

After the men had expressed their thanks as best as they could, Missie began timidly, "Now I want to say thank you for your gift to me."

Five pairs of eyes—six, counting Nathan's—swung to her face. There she sat, just a little scrap of a girl-woman, youthful and pretty, her cheeks glowing with health, her eyes sparkling near tears, her trim figure clothed attractively in a bright calico, the tiny, fair-skinned, chubby-cheeked Nathan contentedly in her arms studying her face.

"I want to thank you," she said shyly, "for workin' so faithfully for my husband, for makin' his load—an' thus mine—easier, for not demandin' things that we can't provide." She hesitated, then smiled, "But most of all, I want to thank you for the good supply of chips that you didn't fuss 'bout haulin'. I've been thankful over an' over for those chips."

Missie couldn't suppress a giggle. Though the men realized that she was sincere in her thankfulness, they also saw the humor in it and gladly laughed with her.

Though unaware of it at that moment, Missie had just made some friends for life. Not one of those men sitting round her tiny shanty would have denied her anything that was in their power to provide.

Later, Henry brought in his guitar and they sang together. Cookie just sat and listened. Sandy whistled a few lines now and then. But Clem, to Missie's surprise, seemed to know by heart most of the traditional carols.

It was hard to break up the little gathering. Several times Missie added more chips to her fire. Little Nathan made the rounds from one pair of arms to another. Even the tough-looking Clem took a turn holding the baby.

At last Missie put the coffeepot back on and boiled a fresh pot. She was glad that she had made enough tarts for each of them to have another one with their coffee.

The men lingered over their tarts and coffee but finally took their leave, tramping their way through the snow back to the bunkhouse.

Missie hummed softly as she washed the dishes—there had been no point trying to find room to wash them earlier. Willie put on his hat and coat and left for the barn, Missie assumed, to check the horses.

Missie had finished the dishes and was feeding Nathan

when Willie returned bearing a box. Missie looked astonished, and he answered her unasked question.

"I did my Christmas shopping 'fore we left Tettsford." He set his box on the table and began to unpack it.

" 'Fraid my gift don't seem too fittin' like in these surroundin's. I was sorta seein' it in our *real* house when I bought it, I guess. Anyway, I thought thet I'd show it to ya, an' then we can sorta pack it off again." Willie lifted from the box the most beautiful fruit bowl that Missie had ever seen.

She gasped, "Willie! It's beautiful."

Willie was relieved when he saw that the bowl had brought her pleasure. He set it gently on the table.

"I'll let ya git a better look at it when yer done with Nathan. Then I'll pack it on back—out of yer way."

"Oh, no," Missie protested. "Just leave it."

She laid the baby on the bed and went to the table to pick up the bowl.

"It's lovely," she said, her fingers caressing it. "Thank you, Willie."

She reached up to kiss him. "An' I don't want you to pack it away—please. It'll be a reminder—an' a promise. I—I need it here. Don't you see?"

Willie held her close. "I see."

After a moment of silence, Willie spoke softly.

"Missie, I wonder—I wonder iffen you'll ever know jest how happy ya made five people today?"

"Five?"

"Those four cowpokes—an' *me*."

Missie's eyes gleamed.

"Then make it *six*, Willie—'cause in doin' what I could, the pleasure all poured right back on me. An' I got the biggest helpin' of happiness myself!"

THE STORY OF THE LOST STAR

Grace Livingston Hill

A bout a week before Christmas in a small city of the East, there appeared in the Lost and Found column this advertisement:

> LOST
>
> *Sometime between the World War and the present morning, The Star of Bethlehem. The finder will confer everlasting favor and receive a reward of ten thousand dollars if returned to the owner between the hours of sundown and midnight on Christmas Eve.*
>
> (Signed) George K. Hamilton,
> Eleven, Harvard Place.

The typesetter blinked and paused in his busy work, read it again, and wondered. Ten thousand dollars! Was it a joke? It must be a mistake! But no, it was paid for. It must go in. He punched away at his machine, and the lines appeared in the type, but his thoughts were busy. Ten thousand dollars! With that he could, with self-respect, marry Mary! He would not have been John if he had not thought of that first.

George K. Hamilton! That was the rich guy who lived in the big house, with one blind wall stuck on its side that everybody said was a picture gallery. He was rolling in wealth, so it must be real. But what was this thing he had lost that was worth everlasting favor and ten thousand dollars? A jewel? A silver tablet? Something of intrinsic historic value perhaps? Something that must be well known, or the writer would not have spoken of it in that offhand, indefinite way as *the* Star of Bethlehem, as if there were but one. Bethlehem—Bethlehem—that was the place where they made steel! Steel! why—steel, of course. George K. Hamilton. Hamilton the steel king! Ah! Why hadn't he thought of it at once?

And why couldn't he go to Bethlehem and find out all about it? He was the first one, excepting the editor of the Lost and Found column, to see this ad. Why wouldn't he stand first chance of the reward if he worked it right?

To be sure there was a possibility that someone, who

knew just what this star was, would be able to get on its track sooner, but if he caught the first train in the morning he would have a good start before anyone read the morning papers.

He would be through with his work by three A.M. at the latest, and there was a train at five. He would have time to get back to his boarding place and clean up a bit, perhaps scribble a note to Mary telling her to be ready for the wedding.

His fingers flew over the keys of his machine as he laid his plans, and his heart throbbed with excitement over the great opportunity that had flung its open door right in his humble path. Ten thousand dollars!

Early dawn saw him dressed in his best and hurrying on his way to Bethlehem amid a trainload of laborers going out for the day's work. But he saw not pick nor shovel nor dinner pail, nor noted greasy overalls and sleepy-eyed companions. Before his shining eyes was a star, sometimes silver, sumptuously engraved, sometimes gold, and set in sparkling jewels, leading him on into the day of adventure.

He essayed to question his fellow seatmate about the star:

"You live in Bethlehem? Did you ever see the Star of Bethlehem?"

But the man stood his head dumbly:

"Me no spak L'angla!"

Arrived in the City of Steel, he went straight to the news agent:

"Have you been here some time?"

"Born here."

"Then tell me, have you a Star of Bethlehem?"

The agent shook his head.

"Don't smoke that kind. Don't keep that kind. Try the little cigar store down the street." And he swung himself under the shelf and, shouldering a pile of morning papers, rushed off down the platform.

Out in the street John stopped a man whose foot was just mounting the running board of his car:

"Do you know anything about the Star of Bethlehem?"

"Never heard of it, man. A Ford's good enough for me!" and he swung into his car and shot away from the curb hurriedly.

He asked a little girl who was hurrying away from the bakery with a basket of bread.

"Why, Star-of-Bethlehem is a flower," she said, "a little green-and-white starry flower with pointed petals. It grows in the meadow over there in the summertime, but it's all gone now. You can't find Stars-of-Bethlehem this time of year!" And she stared after him for a silly fool.

He asked a passer on the street:

"Can you tell me how to find out about Star of Bethlehem?"

The man tapped him lightly on the shoulder with a wink and advised him knowingly, with a thumb pointing down a side alley:

"You better not mention that openly, brother. There's been several raids around here lately, and the police are wise. It ain't safe."

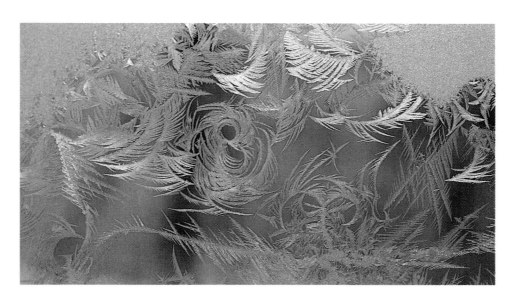

And about this time the Bishop back at home was opening the morning paper at the breakfast table as he toyed with his grapefruit and coffee:

"He, ha!" he said as his eye traveled down the column idly and paused at the Lost and Found, "Listen to this, Bella. Poor old George has got 'em again. He probably thinks he is going to die this time. I'll just step in and have a little talk on theology with him this morning and set his mind at rest. No need for that ten thousand dollars to go out of the church. We might as well have it as some home for the feeble-minded."

Bella left her coffee and came around to read the advertisement, her face lighting intelligently:

"Oh, Basil! Do you think you can work it?" she cried delightedly.

"Why, sure, he's just a little daffy on religion now because he's been sick. The last time I saw him he asked me how we could know any of the creeds were true when they were all so different. I'll smooth it all out for him and make him give another ten thousand or so to the social service work of our church, and he'll come across handsomely, you'll see. I'd better go at once. It won't do to wait, there are too many kinds of crooks on the lookout for just such a soft ten thousand as this." And he took his hat and coat and hurried out.

The Professor at his meager breakfast table, worrying about his sick wife and how he could afford to keep his eldest son in college, happened on the item.

He set down his coffee cup untasted and stepped to his bookshelves, taking down several wise treatises on astronomy.

A sweet-faced saint in an invalid chair read and pondered and murmured thoughtfully: "Poor soul! What's happened to the man's Bible?"

Before night the one little shop in the city that made a specialty of astronomical instruments had been drained of everything in the shape of a searcher of the heavens, and a rush order had gone to New York by telegraph for more telescopes of various sizes and prices, while a boy in the back office who was good at lettering was busy making a copy of the advertisement to fasten up in the plate-glass window, with special electric lights playing about it and a note below:

"Come in and order your telescope now before they are all gone, and get into line for the great sky prize! We have 'em! All prices!"

Far into the evening the crowd continued around that window, and many who had glasses at home hurried away to search for them and build air castles of how they would spend the ten thousand dollars when they got it.

Even before the day was half over, the office of the University was besieged by eager visitors come to question wise ones, a folded newspaper furtively held under each applicant's arm.

As evening drew on, shadowy figures stole forth to high places and might have been seen scanning the heavens and now and then consulting a book by means of a pocket flashlight. More than one young student worked into the small hours of the night with reference books scattered about him, writing a many-paged treatise on the Star of Stars, some to prove that the star was a myth, and others that it was still in existence and would one day appear again as bright as of old. Even the police, coming suddenly upon the lurking stargazers far toward morning, began to question what had taken hold of the town.

Coming home on the late train from a fruitless search for an unknown quantity which was not there, John Powers sat wearily back in the fusty seat of the common car and took out the worn advertisement from his pocket to read it once more.

The lost Star of Bethlehem! What could it be? He had searched the steel city from end to end without finding so much as a trace of tradition or story about a star in connection with that town. He had met with more rebuffs and strange suggestions than ever before in his life together, and he was dog-weary and utterly discouraged. If only he had not written that hopeful letter to Mary in the morning!

Now perhaps she would already be planning to have the wedding soon, and where was the money coming from to provide the little home?

Of course it just might happen that after all the star had been lost up in the city, else why should the advertisement have been put in the city paper and not in the Bethlehem local? But even so, he had hoped great things from this trip to Bethlehem, and now he had only wasted a day and the carfare and had gotten nowhere at all.

At a local station, a loud-mouthed traveler got off, leaving his recent seatmate without anyone to talk to, and presently he joined John Powers and entered into conversation, being one of those men who is never happy unless his tongue is wagging. In the course of their talk, John found himself asking the old question again:

"You say you are from Bethlehem? Did you ever hear of a star in connection with that town? Was there any memorial tablet or monument or emblem or anything in the shape of a star that has been stolen away? Star of Bethlehem it was called, do you know anything about it?"

The stranger stared blankly and shook his head.

"Sounds to me as if it might be a song or a book mebbe. If you knowed who wrote it, you might find out at one o' the schools. My Johnny says you can find out almost anything if you know who wrote it. Ever been a Mason? Might be some kind of a Masonic badge, mightn't it?"

The man got out at the next station, and Powers leaned back wearily and thought how he had failed. His mind seemed too tired to think any longer on the subject.

An old lady with a queer bonnet with many bundles at her feet and a basket beside her, out of which stuck a pair of turkey's feet, leaned over suddenly and touched him on the shoulder.

"Laddie, hae ye tried the auld Buik?" she asked timidly, "I'm thinkin' ye'll find it all there."

"I beg your pardon!" said Powers lifting his hat courteously and thinking how the blue of her eyes had a light like that in Mary's eyes.

He arose from his seat and went back to sit beside her. Then somehow the blue of her eyes made him unafraid, and he told her all about the ten thousand dollars and his fruitless trip to Bethlehem.

"Oh, but laddie, ye're on the wrong track entirely," said the old lady. "The Star of Bethlehem's in the auld Buik. I ken it's no the fashion to read it these days, but the worruld lost sight of a lot besides the things it wanted to forget when it set out to put its Bibles awa! Hunt up yer mither's Bible, lad, and study it out. The star arose in the East ye ken, and the folks who saw it first was those that was lookin' fer its arisin'. The star's *na* lost. It led to the little King ye ken, an' it'll always lead to the King if a body seeks with all the heirt, fer that is the promise: 'An' ye shall find Me, when ye shall seek fer Me with all yer heirts.' Many like the puir buddy who wrote the bit lines in the paper was longin' fer the King hisself an' wanted the star to guide him, but ye ken ye can't purchase the gifts of God wi' silver ner gold. The mon may lay his ten thousand baubles at the fut of the throne, but he'll find he must go his own self across the desert, and wait mayhap, before he'll ever see the shinin' of the Star. But you'll not turn back yerself now you've started, laddie! Go find the King fer yerself. Look in the Gospels an' read the story. It's passin' wonderful an' lovely. This is my station now, and I'll be leavin' ye, but it'll be a glad Christmas time fer you ef you find the little King, an' *ye'll find Him sure,* if ye seek with all yer heirt."

The doorway to the fine old Hamilton mansion on Harvard Place was besieged by applicants from morning to night all that week, wishing to speak with the Master, but to all, the grave and dignified servitor who answered the door replied:

"My master is away. He cannot speak with you until the time appointed. If any then have found the lost treasure, they may come and claim the reward. But they must come bringing it with them. None others need present themselves."

Even the Bishop had not been able to gain admittance. He was much annoyed about it. He was afraid others would get ahead of him. He had written a letter, but he knew it had not yet been opened, for the last time he called he had seen it lying on the console in the hall with a lot of other unopened letters. The Bishop was very certain that if he could have audience *first,* all would be well. He was sure he could explain the philosophy of life and the mystery of the star quite satisfactorily and soothingly.

Before John Powers had gone back to work that night on his return from Bethlehem, he had gone to the bottom of an old chest and hunted out his mother's Bible. It was worn and dropping apart in places, but he put it tenderly on his bed, and following an impulse, dropped to his knees beside it, laying his lips against its dusty covers. Somehow the very look of the old worn covers brought back his childhood days and a sense of sin in that he had wandered so far from the path in which his mother had set his young feet.

All that week he gave all the extra time he had to studying about the star. He did not even go to see Mary. He lost sight of the ten thousand dollars in his interest in the star itself. He was now seeking to find that star for himself, not for the reward that had been offered. He wanted to find the King who was also a Saviour.

The last night before it came time for him to go to his work, he dropped upon his knees once more beside the little tattered book and prayed:

"Oh Jesus Christ, Saviour of the world, I thank Thee that Thou has sent Thy star to guide me to Thee. I worship Thee, and I give myself to Thee forever."

On Christmas Eve, when the door of the mansion was thrown open, a large throng of people entered and were speedily admitted, one by one, to audience with the master of the house, until in an incredibly short space of time, the waiting room was emptied of philosophers and dreamers and ambitious ones. Even the Bishop had been courteously sent his way. Only three were left. Three wise ones, and two of them were women!

One was an old woman with a burr upon her tongue and a Bible in her hand; one was a young girl with blue, starry eyes and a bit of a Testament in the folds of her gown where she kept her fingers between the leaves to a place. The third was John Powers, standing within the shadow of a heavy curtain beside a deepset window looking out at the great shining of a bright star, with peace upon his face. He turned about as the door closed after the Bishop and glanced at the two women. The girl looked up and their eyes met.

"Mary!"

"John!"

There was scarcely time to recognize the old woman before the door opened and George K. Hamilton, keen of eye, sharp of feature, eager of expression, walked in and looked from one to the other, searching each face questioningly.

The young man stepped forward to meet him, and Mary saw for the first time that a worn little Bible was in his hand.

But John was speaking in such a ringing voice of certainty:

"Sir, I want to tell you first that I have not come for your money. When I began this search, it was in hope of the reward, but I've found the Star itself, and it led me to the King, and now I've brought it to you because I want you to have it too. You'll find it in this Book. It has to be searched for, but it's there. And when you have found it, I've been thinking you'll maybe want to sell all that you have and give to the poor and go and follow *Him*. But *I* am not one of those poor any longer, for I *have found the King!* Come, Mary, shall we go?"

Then up rose the old Scotch woman from her place near the door:

"I've just one more word to say, an' ye'll find it in yon Buik: 'Arise, shine; for thy light is come, and the Glory of the Lord is risen upon thee.' That star isn't lost, sir, an' never was! Never will be! It's up in the heavens waiting till the King has need of it again, and someday it will burst upon the world again and they will all know that it has been there all the time!"

The Master was left alone in his mansion with the book in his hand and a strange awed feeling of the Presence of God in his room.

He looked wonderingly, doubtfully, down at the book and then wistfully out through his richly draped window to where a single star shone softly through the Christmas night.

"A MERRY CHRISTMAS"

from

LITTLE WOMEN

Louisa May Alcott

Jo was the first to wake in the gray dawn of Christmas morning. No stockings hung at the fireplace, and for a moment she felt as much disappointed as she did long ago, when her little sock fell down because it was so crammed with goodies. Then she remembered her mother's promise and, slipping her hand under her pillow, drew out a little crimson-covered book. She knew it very well, for it was that beautiful old story of the best life ever lived, and Jo felt that it was a true guidebook for any pilgrim going the long journey. She woke Meg with a "Merry Christmas" and bade her see what was under her pillow. A green-covered book appeared with the same picture inside and a few words written by their mother, which made their one present very precious in their eyes. Presently Beth and Amy woke to rummage and find their little books also—one dove-colored, the other blue; and all sat looking at and talking about them while the east grew rosy with the coming day.

In spite of her small vanities, Margaret had a sweet and pious nature, which unconsciously influenced her sisters, especially Jo, who loved her very tenderly and obeyed her because her advice was so gently given.

"Girls," said Meg seriously, looking from the tumbled head beside her to the two little night-capped ones in the room beyond, "mother wants us to read and love and mind these books, and we must begin at once. We used to be faithful about it, but since father went away and all this war trouble unsettled us, we have neglected many things. You can do as you please, but *I* shall keep my book on the table here and read a little every morning as soon as I wake, for I know it will do me good and help me through the day."

Then she opened her new book and began to read. Jo put her arm round her and, leaning cheek to cheek, read also, with the quiet expression so seldom seen on her restless face.

"How good Meg is! Come, Amy, let's do as they do. I'll help you with the hard words, and they'll explain things if we don't understand," whispered Beth, very much impressed by the pretty books and her sisters' example.

"I'm glad mine is blue," said Amy, and then the rooms were very still while the pages softly turned, and the winter sunshine crept in to touch the bright heads and serious faces with a Christmas greeting.

"Where is mother?" asked Meg, as she and Jo ran down to thank her for their gifts half an hour later.

"Goodness only knows. Some poor creeter come a-beggin', and your ma went straight off to see what was needed. There never *was* such a woman for givin' away vittles and drink, clothes and firin'," replied Hannah, who had lived with the family since Meg was born and was considered by them all more as a friend than a servant.

"She will be back soon, I think, so fry your cakes, and have everything ready," said Meg, looking over the presents, which were collected in a basket and kept under the sofa, ready to be produced at the proper time. "Why, where is Amy's bottle of cologne?" she added, as the little flask did not appear.

"She took it out a minute ago and went off with it to put a ribbon on it, or some such notion," replied Jo, dancing about the room to take the first stiffness off the new army-slippers.

"How nice my handkerchiefs look, don't they? Hannah

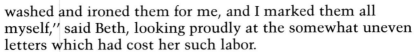

washed and ironed them for me, and I marked them all myself," said Beth, looking proudly at the somewhat uneven letters which had cost her such labor.

"Bless the child! she's gone and put 'Mother' on them instead of 'M. March.' How funny!" cried Jo, taking up one.

"Isn't it right? I thought it was better to do it so, because Meg's initials are 'M.M.,' and I don't want any one to use these but Marmee," said Beth, looking troubled.

"It's all right, dear, and a very pretty idea—quite sensible, too, for no one can ever mistake now. It will please her very much, I know," said Meg, with a frown for Jo and a smile for Beth.

"There's mother. Hide the basket, quick!" cried Jo, as a door slammed and steps sounded in the hall.

Amy came in hastily and looked rather abashed when she saw her sisters all waiting for her.

"Where have you been, and what are you hiding behind you?" asked Meg, surprised to see, by her hood and cloak, that lazy Amy had been out so early.

"Don't laugh at me, Jo! I didn't mean anyone should know till the time came. I only meant to change the little bottle for a big one, and I gave *all* my money to get it, and I'm truly trying not to be selfish any more."

As she spoke, Amy showed the handsome flask which replaced the cheap one and looked so earnest and humble in her little effort to forget herself that Meg hugged her on the spot and Jo pronounced her "a trump," while Beth ran to the window and picked her finest rose to ornament the stately bottle.

"You see, I felt ashamed of my present, after reading and talking about being good this morning, so I ran round the corner and changed it the minute I was up, and I'm *so* glad, for mine is the handsomest now."

Another bang of the street door sent the basket under the sofa and the girls to the table, eager for breakfast.

"Merry Christmas, Marmee! Many of them! Thank you for our books; we read some and mean to every day," they cried, in chorus.

"Merry Christmas, little daughters! I'm glad you began at once and hope you will keep on. But I want to say one word before we sit down. Not far away from here lies a poor woman with a little newborn baby. Six children are huddled into one bed to keep from freezing, for they have no fire. There is nothing to eat over there, and the oldest boy came to tell me they were suffering hunger and cold. My girls, will you give them your breakfast as a Christmas present?"

They were all unusually hungry, having waited nearly an hour, and for a minute no one spoke; only a minute, for Jo exclaimed impetuously—

"I'm so glad you came before we began!"

"May I go and help carry the things to the poor little children?" asked Beth eagerly.

"*I* shall take the cream and the muffins," added Amy, heroically giving up the articles she most liked.

Meg was already covering the buckwheats and piling the bread into one big plate.

"I thought you'd do it," said Mrs. March, smiling as if satisfied. "You shall all go and help me, and when we come

back we will have bread and milk for breakfast and make it up at dinnertime."

They were soon ready, and the procession set out. Fortunately it was early, and they went through back streets, so few people saw them, and no one laughed at the queer party.

A poor, bare, miserable room it was, with broken windows, no fire, ragged bedclothes, a sick mother, wailing baby, and a group of pale, hungry children cuddled under one old quilt, trying to keep warm.

How the big eyes stared and the blue lips smiled as the girls went in!

"Ach, mein Gott! it is good angels come to us!" said the poor woman, crying for joy.

"Funny angels in hoods and mittens," said Jo, and set them laughing.

In a few minutes it really did seem as if kind spirits had been at work there. Hannah, who had carried wood, made a fire and stopped up the broken panes with old hats and her own cloak. Mrs. March gave the mother tea and gruel and comforted her with promises of help, while she dressed the little baby as tenderly as if it had been her own. The girls, meantime, spread the table, set the children round the fire, and fed them like so many hungry birds—laughing, talking, and trying to understand the funny broken English.

"Das ist gut!" "Die Engel-kinder!" cried the poor things as they ate and warmed their purple hands at the comfortable blaze.

The girls had never been called angel children before and thought it very agreeable, especially Jo, who had been considered a "Sancho" ever since she was born. That was a very happy breakfast, though they didn't get any of it, and when they went away, leaving comfort behind, I think there were not in all the city four merrier people than the hungry little girls who gave away their breakfasts and contented themselves with bread and milk on Christmas morning.

"That's loving our neighbor better than ourselves, and I like it," said Meg, as they set out their presents, while their mother was upstairs collecting clothes for the poor Hummels.

Not a very splendid show, but there was a great deal of love done up in the few little bundles, and the tall vase of red roses, white chrysanthemums, and trailing vines, which stood in the middle, gave quite an elegant air to the table.

"She's coming! Strike up, Beth! Open the door, Amy! Three cheers for Marmee!" cried Jo, prancing about, while Meg went to conduct mother to the seat of honor.

Beth played her gayest march, Amy threw open the door, and Meg enacted escort with great dignity. Mrs. March was both surprised and touched and smiled with her eyes full as she examined her presents and read the little notes which accompanied them. The slippers went on at once, a new handkerchief was slipped into her pocket, well scented with Amy's cologne, the rose was fastened in her bosom, and the nice gloves were pronounced a "perfect fit."

There was a good deal of laughing and kissing and explaining in the simple, loving fashion which makes these home festivals so pleasant at the time, so sweet to remember long afterward....

THE MIRACULOUS STAIRCASE

Arthur Gordon

On that cool December morning in 1878, sunlight lay like an amber rug across the dusty streets and adobe houses of Santa Fe. It glinted on the bright tile roof of the almost completed Chapel of Our Lady of Light and on the nearby windows of the convent school run by the Sisters of Loretto. Inside the convent, the Mother Superior looked up from her packing as a tap came on her door.

"It's *another* carpenter, Reverend Mother," said Sister Francis Louise, her round face apologetic. "I told him that you're leaving right away, that you haven't time to see him, but he says..."

"I know what he says," Mother Magdalene said, going on resolutely with her packing. "That he's heard about our

THE CHRISTMAS IN MAMA'S KITCHEN

Jean Bell Mosley

For years, we put the Christmas tree in the parlor. It was the fanciest room in the old farmhouse—carpeted, wallpapered, and curtained. It seemed fitting to celebrate the Master's birthday in the best room.

However, there was too much activity going on from day to day in the big kitchen—Mama's kitchen—to maintain an unused fire elsewhere, so there wasn't always a fire burning in the parlor. Grandma and Mama cooked, sewed, churned, washed, and ironed in the kitchen. Dad and Grandpa kept their accounts, read the papers, soled shoes there. My two sisters and I did homework, helped with the chores, played our games there. Mama's kitchen fireplace was always aglow, the range constantly fired. It was a big spacious room—bright and cozy.

On December Sundays or special holidays, when company was expected, Dad would make a fire in the parlor stove and we'd all go in to enjoy the tree, breathe its cedary fragrance, touch the old familiar baubles. Baby Jesus, in his crib in the crèche beneath the tree, would, after a long time, feel warm to our touch.

But somehow the parlor never had the coziness Mama's kitchen had. I always liked the big center table we gathered around, face to face, making small talk or sometimes serious talk. If Mama read a Christmas story aloud in the parlor, it wasn't the same as in the kitchen accompanied by the sputtering fireplace and singing teakettle. Even our evening prayers seemed to come naturally in the kitchen.

One winter evening, as the fire died in the parlor stove, I boldly lifted the crib from the crèche and took it into the kitchen, setting it near the fireplace. My sisters, thinking I had been irreverent, told Mama.

"Let it be," Mama said. She smiled at me, though I had expected a reprimand.

The next Christmas, when Dad and Grandpa brought the tree home, Mama said, "I mean to put it up here in the kitchen this year."

"Celebrate His birthday in here with the smell of cabbage cooking, the butter being churned, our old barn clothes

hanging over there?" one of my sisters demanded.

"Let's try it," Mama said.

The hat rack was moved a little closer to the sewing machine. The cot was pushed up against another wall to make room. When we came downstairs for breakfast, in from the outdoor chores, home from school, there was the tree, bright, warm, and fragrant. We trimmed it leisurely—cranberry chains one evening, popcorn garlands the next. Baby Jesus, in the crib, close and dear, was always warm, as were the little sheep, donkeys, shepherds, and Wise Men.

When we read the Christmas story, starting seven nights before Christmas so each could have his turn at reading it, the event that happened so long ago and far away now seemed so close, as if it might have happened just last night in our own cow stable. I could visualize the Baby lying in Star's haylined feed box; hear the soft, velvety whinny of Dobbin looking on through the bars; the stirrings of other creatures that had come in from the cold.

The moon and stars that the shepherds saw that night in their pastures were the same moon and stars that shone on me when I went to close the chicken-house door. White-bearded Grandpa, coming in from the snowy outdoors, bearing a gift of shiny red apples from the apple hole, looked very much like a Wise Man. We didn't know what had happened to our

Christmas, but we knew it was better than any we'd ever had.

One afternoon a neighbor dropped in with some cookies. "Why, Myrtle," she said to Mama, "is this—is—this—appropriate—" Her voice trailed off. But after looking around

the kitchen her face lit up. "Myrtle," she exclaimed, "you've brought Christmas in here to be an everyday thing, warm and comfortable, right amongst your living!"

Mama smiled and replied, "Only our best for the Master." She may have winked at me. I don't know. Fireplace shadows sometimes play tricks, and holiday eyes get so bright they have to blink often.

FARAWAY CHRISTMAS

Norman Vincent Peale

Golden stars and angels. Festive lights and carols. Shoppers with gaily wrapped packages. Windows glowing with Yuletide pageantry. "Oh," a friend said to me, "aren't they wonderful, all these warm, familiar symbols? Christmas wouldn't be Christmas without them!"

I had to smile a little. Let me tell you why.

Not too long ago, my wife Ruth and the other members of our family, our three children and spouses with assorted grandchildren, persuaded me that it would be a great adventure to spend Christmas in a completely different setting, one with a totally new atmosphere. "What if we went to Africa," they said with great excitement, "and lived in tents in one of those game parks surrounded by all those wonderful animals? Wouldn't a faraway Christmas be exciting? Wouldn't it be terrific? Wouldn't family ties be strengthened by such a unique experience?"

I protested feebly that perhaps someone who had passed his eighty-seventh birthday, as I had, might find living in a tent surrounded by wild animals a bit strenuous. But no one seemed to be listening. "You'll love every minute of it," Ruth assured me. And so on this high note of excitement and enthusiasm, we made our preparations to go to East Africa.

The Samburu Game Park in Kenya was indeed far away. And indeed it was different. Ruth and I shared a tent pitched near a fast-flowing, brown river. In tents on either side were our children and grandchildren. There was heat and dust and burning sun. At night the forest resounded with barks, screeches, splashes, and once, just behind our tents, a grunting sound that they told me next day had probably been made by a leopard.

So I did not sleep very well, but these unfamiliar things were not what troubled me. What troubled me was that nothing seemed like Christmas. I tried to shrug off the feeling, but it persisted, a kind of emptiness, a sadness almost, a small voice that whispered, "Christmas means coming home, doesn't it? Why have all of you chosen to turn your backs on home like this?" I did my best to conceal such thoughts from the others, but I could not conceal them from myself. And they kept coming back, often at unexpected moments.

On the afternoon of Christmas Eve, for example, we had come back from a splendid day of viewing the animals. We had seen a beautiful herd of zebras, seventy-six elephants, a cheetah chasing an impala, a nursing lioness, all magnificent in their natural surroundings. Then it was time for a shower before dinner, which was a bit of an adventure, too. The camp helpers heated water, put it in a bucket, then hoisted the

bucket to the top of a pole behind the tent. From there the water ran down a pipe into the rear of the tent where, standing on slats, the bather could soap and rinse himself. After a fashion.

I was drying myself off when suddenly—I don't know what triggered it—I found myself remembering long ago Christmases spent in Cincinnati during my impressionable boyhood years. The city was full of people of German descent, and the Germans are very sentimental about Christmas. I found myself recalling Fountain Square as it looked on Christmas Eve; I thought it the biggest, brightest, most beautiful place I had ever seen. The Christmas tree was enormous, and the streets were alive with carols, many sung in German: "Stille Nacht" and "O Tannenbaum." I could see myself walking with my father, my small hand in his big one, the snow crunching under our feet. Up on East Liberty Street, where we lived, my mother always had a tree with real candles on it. The smell of those tallow candles mingled with the scent of fir, an aroma unlike any other. Now, standing in our little tent with the vastness of Africa all around me, I remembered that wonderful smell, and I missed it terribly.

We had been told that there would be a special dinner for us that evening. Even this did not cheer me; I thought it might be an artificial occasion with everyone trying too hard to be merry. When I came out near dinnertime, I saw that in the

eating tent a straggly brown bush had been set up, decorated with small colored lights and some tinsel and red ribbon. I thought of the great tree in Fountain Square and the even greater one in Rockefeller Center in New York City or the magnificent one on the great lawn of the White House.

We were called to the edge of the river where chairs had been set up for all of us so that we could see, on the other side, two herders guarding their cattle, their spear tips gleaming like points of light in the gathering dusk. And at that peaceful, almost timeless sight, I felt something stir within me, for I knew that these herders and their charges had not changed in thousands of years. They belonged to their landscape just as the shepherds on the hills outside Bethlehem belonged to theirs. And at that moment one of the grandchildren began to sing, hesitantly, tentatively, "O Little Town of Bethlehem." Gradually others joined in: "Hark the Herald Angels," and then "Joy to the World." Soon we were all singing, and as we sang everything seemed to change; the sense of strangeness was gone. I looked around the group, our children, their children, singing songs, sharing feelings that in a very real way went back almost two thousand years to that simple manger in a simple town, with the herders standing by in a parched and primitive land.

Then someone began to read the immortal story from Luke: "And there were in the same country shepherds abiding in the field, keeping watch over their flock by night...." As the story went on, I thought, *How wonderful and simple it is, so wonderful and simple that only God could have thought of it.*

I found myself remembering a radio talk given many years ago by Sam Shoemaker, a much loved pastor and a good friend of mine. In it Sam was speculating on what God the Father might have said to Jesus His Son on the night before Jesus left Him to go down to earth. He imagined Father and Son conversing much as a human boy and his father might do before the son leaves home to go out into the world. Only Sam with his great simplicity could picture it this way. According to this conception, God might have said, "Son, I hate to see You go. I sure am going to miss You. I love You with all My heart. But I do want You to go down to earth and tell those poor souls down there how to live and point them to the way that will lead them back home."

Sam said he thought the last thing God said to Jesus was, "Give them all My love." Now that is simple, but it's human and it's divine.

So when the carols and the Bible reading ended and we walked back to the eating tent for our dinner, I knew with a complete sense of peace that where Christmas is concerned, surroundings do not matter, because the spirit of Jesus is everywhere, knocking on the door of our hearts, asking to be taken in.

The festive lights and the gifts and the ornaments are fine, but they are only a setting for the real jewel: the birth of a Baby that marked the descent of God Himself to mankind. That is where the true meaning of Christmas lies. And it can be found in that simple sentence: "Give them all My love."

TROUBLE AT THE INN

Dina Donohue

For years now whenever Christmas pageants are talked about in a certain little town in the Midwest, someone is sure to mention the name of Wallace Purling. Wally's performance in one annual production of the Nativity play has slipped into the realm of legend. But the old-timers who were in the audience that night never tire of recalling exactly what happened.

Wally was nine that year and in the second grade, though he should have been in the fourth. Most people in town knew that he had difficulty in keeping up. He was big and clumsy, slow in movement and mind. Still, Wally was well liked by the other children in his class, all of whom were smaller than he, though the boys had trouble hiding their irritation when Wally would ask to play ball with them or any game, for that matter, in which winning was important.

Most often they'd find a way to keep him out, but Wally would hang around anyway—not sulking, just hoping. He was always a helpful boy, a willing and smiling one, and the natural protector, paradoxically, of the underdog. If the older boys chased the younger ones away, it would always be Wally who'd say, "Can't they stay? They're no bother."

Wally fancied the idea of being a shepherd with a flute in the Christmas pageant that year, but the play's director, Miss Lumbard, assigned him to a more important role. After all, she reasoned, the Innkeeper did not have too many lines, and Wally's size would make his refusal of lodging to Joseph more forceful.

And so it happened that the usual large, partisan audience gathered for the town's yearly extravaganza of crooks and crèches, of beards, crowns, halos, and a whole stage full of squeaky voices. No one on stage or off was more caught up in the magic of the night than Wallace Purling. They said later that he stood in the wings and watched the performance with such fascination that from time to time Miss Lumbard had to make sure he didn't wander onstage before his cue.

Then the time came when Joseph appeared, slowly, tenderly guiding Mary to the door of the inn. Joseph knocked hard on the wooden door set into the painted backdrop. Wally the Innkeeper was there, waiting.

"What do you want?" Wally said, swinging the door open

with a brusque gesture.

"We seek lodging."

"Seek it elsewhere." Wally looked straight ahead but spoke vigorously. "The inn is filled."

"Sir, we have asked everywhere in vain. We have traveled far and are very weary."

"There is no room in this inn for you." Wally looked properly stern.

"Please, good Innkeeper, this is my wife, Mary. She is heavy with child and needs a place to rest. Surely you must have some small corner for her. She is so tired."

Now, for the first time, the Innkeeper relaxed his stiff stance and looked down at Mary. With that, there was a long pause, long enough to make the audience a bit tense with embarrassment.

"No! Begone!" the prompter whispered from the wings.

"No!" Wally repeated automatically. "Begone!"

Joseph sadly placed his arm around Mary, and Mary laid her head upon her husband's shoulder, and the two of them started to move away. The Innkeeper did not return inside his inn, however. Wally stood there in the doorway, watching the

forlorn couple. His mouth was open, his brow creased with concern, his eyes filling unmistakably with tears.

And suddenly this Christmas pageant became different from all others.

"Don't go, Joseph," Wally called out. "Bring Mary back." And Wallace Purling's face grew into a bright smile. "You can have my room."

Some people in town thought that the pageant had been ruined. Yet there were others—many, many others—who considered it the most Christmas of all Christmas pageants they had ever seen.

STARR AND THE MAGIC CHRISTMAS BOX

Marilyn Morgan Helleberg

"It's Christmas Box Day! It's Christmas Box Day!" shouted seven-year-old Starr as she bounced out the school door, dragging her new coat across the melting ice.

"Starr! Put on your coat or I'll tell Moms," scolded Stephanie, who was twelve and stepping carefully around the wet spots.

Starr slipped into her coat without slowing down for her big sister. She could hardly wait to get home so the magic could begin! Every year, for as long as she could remember, the day school got out for the holidays had been Christmas Box Day. On that day, Moms would pull down the attic ladder and climb through the dusty openings. Then, while Starr and Stephanie waited breathlessly in the closet below, they'd hear a *creak, creak*, as the trunk lid opened and closed. Then *crick, crick*, as she wound up the music box, and finally, just when they couldn't stand the suspense any longer, the magic tune would begin...

Silent night, Holy night....

Moms would step back through the opening and place the magic box on the coffee table where the girls could watch the delicate angel dance around and around on the shiny glass. Always, just at that moment, Christmas would begin at the Shorewoods' house.

Daddy had made the angel himself and rigged her to the wind-up mechanism so that she would dance as the music played. Even now, Starr could see a picture in her mind of her tall, gangly, dark-eyed, curly-haired father with that funny little mole on his cheek at the edge of his mustache. She could see him sitting at the kitchen table with his magnifying glass and tweezers, humming in his usual off-key way, as he worked his magic. Because it *was* a magical thing, the way he had created the angel out of delicate shells from the family's seaside vacation, using tiny wires, glue, and an infinite supply of love and patience. It wasn't really surprising, though. At least not to Starr. She was sure there wasn't anything Daddy couldn't do.

121

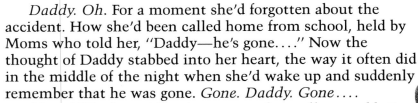

Daddy. Oh. For a moment she'd forgotten about the accident. How she'd been called home from school, held by Moms who told her, "Daddy—he's gone...." Now the thought of Daddy stabbed into her heart, the way it often did in the middle of the night when she'd wake up and suddenly remember that he was gone. *Gone. Daddy. Gone....*

"Starr! Watch out! Don't get your shoes all...muddy." Too late. Starr could feel the cool, watery mud slishing in over the middle of her right shoe. She looked down at her own already scuffed shoes, then at Stephanie's shiny, new-looking ones. "Well, I couldn't help it, Steffie. I was thinking about the magic Christmas box and..."

"Magic! Good grief, Starr. Why don't you grow up? There's no such thing as magic! Besides, I think we ought to leave the box in the attic this year, because...well, just because." Stephanie pulled her sister over to the damp grass to wipe off her shoe. "And quit calling me Steffie. I'm not a little kid any more, like you. My name's Stephanie."

Things got blurry then. Starr blinked. Hard. No Christmas box? No magic? Then suddenly, from somewhere deep in her stomach, something sharp and fiery shot all the way through her and out the top of her head. "There *is too* magic in the Christmas box! There is! There is!"

Stephanie walked on ahead, her back stiff, her hands fisted to whiteness.

The fiery feeling Starr had had a moment ago turned to gray ice inside of her. The magic was gone. Nothing else mattered. "I guess you're right," Starr muttered, studying the sidewalk, and followed her sister into the house.

Moms was on the phone and didn't hear the girls come in. "Well, I'm not sending out any cards this year. Tree? Oh, I suppose we'll have to put up something. I'll do it for the sake of the girls. And the thought of no one to talk over what to get the girls...To tell you the truth, Nancy, this year I just want Christmas to be over with!"

Starr drew in a thin little breath and tiptoed into her room. She wouldn't mention the Christmas box. No. Not this year.

On Christmas Eve, Moms's friend Nancy brought over a small, artificial Christmas tree, and Starr and Stephanie and Moms decorated it, but they didn't gather around the piano afterwards for the family carol-sing. Just thinking about that brought Starr another stab in the chest. She could almost hear Daddy singing, off-key as always, at the top of his voice, and loving every minute of it. Then Starr thought about Daddy's usual reply to the family's teasing: "Well, the *piano* must be out of tune!" How they all laughed every time he said it! Even now, a small chuckle escaped, as Starr remembered.

"Well," said Moms, "the tree is done. I think we all need to get to bed."

Snapped back to reality, Starr kissed Moms and then went to her room, closed the door, and got ready for bed. She tried to sleep but couldn't make her eyes stay closed. Every night she missed her Daddy, and tonight being Christmas Eve, she

missed him most. "Please, God," Starr prayed silently, echoing Moms's words, "just let Christmas be over with." Then, from somewhere in the dark, she seemed to hear a voice. It sounded steady and sure: "Starr! The Christmas box. Go get it!"

Very quietly, Starr tiptoed into her closet and closed the door before turning on the light. She'd never pulled the ladder down by herself before, but she stood as tall as she could and reached as high as she could, and the tip of her middle finger caught the edge of it. Down it came, and she stopped it just before it reached the floor, letting it down noiselessly. Then up she climbed, with her flashlight. It was the scariest thing she'd ever done, but she had to do it. She opened the old trunk and looked inside. There it was! As Starr took off the tissue paper Moms had wrapped it in, gently fingering the delicate shells of the angel, her satin dress and feathered wings, a little tickle started up inside of her, right between her ribs. But she didn't wind up the music box. She didn't dare. It was enough just to see and hold it. She'd keep it under the covers at night and hide it on the shelves behind her dolls in the daytime, and maybe, just maybe, it could still work its magic in this house.

Starr started back down the ladder, holding the music box close to her heart. Then suddenly, her left foot missed a rung! She felt the Christmas box fly out of her hands as she crashed, *slam-bang*, on the hard closet floor. *Crash-clatter-shatter!* Oh No! Oh No! The Christmas box! Starr looked around her and saw pieces of broken seashells! Shattered glass! Bent springs! Then they all blurred together as her eyes filled with hot, stinging tears.

In the next moment, Moms and Stephanie came running

in. "What happened? Starr! Are you all right?"

"Oh, Mommy, Mommy! The Christmas box! Daddy's magic Christmas box! I'm so sorry. Oh, Mommy!"

Moms picked her little girl up in her arms and held her, rocking back and forth, smoothing Starr's hair. "It's okay, honey. It's okay. You didn't mean to do it."

Starr expected her sister to scream at her about being clumsy. What happened was almost worse. Without a word, Stephanie picked up the broken pieces of the music box and carried them quietly out of the room.

Starr noticed that Moms's eyes were red, as she tucked her into bed with a kiss and went out, closing the door softly behind her. Starr buried her head in her pillow and sobbed until she fell asleep.

When she woke up, it was Christmas morning, and for a few brief moments, she felt the old tingle of excitement. Then she remembered, and the gray sadness crept over her again. How could she ever have believed in anything magical? Suddenly, more than anything else, she just wanted Christmas to be over with!

Then, from somewhere far, far away, she heard the twinkling sound of a familiar song.

Silent night, Holy night. . . .

Starr blinked her eyes. She *had* to be dreaming. The music box was broken. She knew that. She sat up in bed and listened. But wait. There was the sound again. She stepped out onto the cold oak floor, put on her slippers, and peeked out her bedroom door. There, on the dining-room table, was Daddy's Christmas music box. And look! The little angel was all put together and dancing again! Afraid to believe it, Starr looked at Moms.

"Stephanie stayed up most of the night putting it all back together for you, Starr. It's almost as good as new!"

Shocked, Starr looked at her older sister.

"I knew how much it meant to you," was all that Stephanie could say. And in that very moment, the magic of Christmas came back to the Shorewood house.

As Starr and Stephanie and Moms watched the angel and listened to her song, they noticed a strange thing. Something was wrong. The notes were just ever-so-slightly off key!

Suddenly, Moms burst out laughing. "The *piano* must be out of tune!" she said. And the three of them laughed and hugged and laughed till the tears ran down their cheeks.

A MODERN-DAY
CHRISTMAS CAROL

Van Varner

When Christmas comes to the city, same as everywhere, some of us do some peculiar things. One year I sent a Christmas card to a shopkeeper. But first let me explain....

You see, New York City is really a large collection of small villages. We reside in tiny territories with boundaries shaped by the shops, churches, schools, cafés, and movie houses that we frequent. It doesn't take long to recognize the face behind the counter at the dry cleaner's and the open-'til-midnight deli. Soon the news vendor by the subway is saying "Hi," and after a while, the florist throws in an extra stem or two. We're not overly friendly with one another, but I think in our little city-spheres, familiarity breeds *contentment*.

When I lived in another part of the city, however, there was one shopkeeper who was not only unfriendly, he was downright mean. He sold lumber (I was always building bookshelves and things in those days), and he'd cut it to exact sizes. He never looked at me when I'd present my order, and any replies were always curt. He'd grunt and grimace and act as if he were doing me a big favor. I didn't like going in there, but his was the only lumber shop in the neighborhood.

To this day I cannot tell you specifically why, but one year as Christmas approached, I sent him a Christmas card. (And something you should know about me—I *never* send Christmas cards.) "Thank you for the good lumber you sold me this year," I wrote on it. Then mailed it and promptly forgot about it.

Months later I needed to go to the lumber loft again. I guess I shouldn't have been surprised—the man was the same. Cold. Not a word was said, and again he didn't look at me. I watched him draw a two-by-four from the stacks, cut it, and tie the pieces together. Then he took my money and gave me my receipt. I was almost out the door when I heard, "Mr. Varner..."

I turned, startled to hear my name. The shopkeeper was standing by his cutting machine. This time he was looking straight at me. At last he spoke.

"Come again," he said softly.

Didn't I say we do peculiar things at Christmas? We seek out relatives who bore us. We spend money we do not have. We send cards to people we don't like. Why? Because we are not ourselves at Christmas. It is one brief time when we become what we want to be but are too busy or too stingy or too embarrassed to be the rest of the year: sentimental, forgiving, forbearing, generous, overgenerous, thoughtful, appreciative of others.

Jesus came, He said, that we might have life and have it more abundantly. And this is so at Christmas, the anniversary of His birth, when in some beautiful, mysterious way, we live beyond ourselves.

CHRISTMAS
IN THE
SOUTH PACIFIC

Glenn Kittler

During World War II, I was stationed on a South Pacific island. Although Christmas was approaching, the nighttime temperature rarely fell below eighty degrees. We swam almost every day, and wildflowers and flamboyant trees were in brilliant blossom. To add to this, the tragedy of the war made it difficult for us to feel the least Christmas spirit.

But then a big box arrived from home. In it my mother had sent all the figurines for a crèche: the Mother and Child, Joseph, the shepherds, angels, the animals, each carefully packed in sawdust and wood shavings.

Immediately I took the box over to the makeshift chapel we had built from scraps. The chaplain and a couple of my buddies were there, and together we built a stagelike box of plywood, scorching it and varnishing it, then installing a tiny lighting system. On Christmas Eve we collected some straw and wildflowers and small branches for the interior of the box. Then we set the figurines in place, just as we had so often seen them back home. When the men—Americans of almost every faith and creed—arrived for Christmas Eve services, you should have seen the joy and wonder that lit up their eyes.

Was it Christmas? Yes, it certainly was. Our crèche was a sturdy symbol of God's reaching out into a strange and dangerous place. Just as His Presence was with the Christ Child in Bethlehem long ago, so it was there in our hearts in the South Pacific.

THE MAN WHO MISSED CHRISTMAS

J. Edgar Parks

It was Christmas Eve, and, as usual, George Mason was the last to leave the office. He walked over to a massive safe, spun the dials, swung the heavy door open. Making sure the door would not close behind him, he stepped inside.

A square of white cardboard was taped just above the topmost row of strongboxes. On the card a few words were written. George Mason stared at those words, remembering...

Exactly one year ago he had entered this self-same vault. And then, behind his back, slowly, noiselessly, the ponderous door swung shut. He was trapped—entombed in the sudden and terrifying dark.

He hurled himself at the unyielding door, his hoarse cry sounding like an explosion. Through his mind flashed all the stories he had heard of men found suffocated in time-vaults. No timeclock controlled this mechanism; the safe would remain locked until it was opened from the outside. Tomorrow morning.

Then the realization hit him. No one would come tomorrow—tomorrow was Christmas.

Once more he flung himself at the door, shouting wildly, until he sank on his knees exhausted. Silence came, high-pitched, singing silence that seemed deafening. More than thirty-six hours would pass before anyone came—thirty-six hours in a steel box three feet wide, eight feet long, seven feet high. Would the oxygen last? Perspiring and breathing heavily, he felt his way around the floor. Then, in the far

right-hand corner, just above the floor, he found a small, circular opening. Quickly he thrust his finger into it and felt, faint but unmistakable, a cool current of air.

The tension release was so sudden that he burst into tears. But at last he sat up. Surely he would not have to stay trapped for the full thirty-six hours. Somebody would miss him.

But who? He was unmarried and lived alone. The maid who cleaned his apartment was just a servant; he had always treated her as such. He had been invited to spend Christmas Eve with his brother's family, but children got on his nerves and expected presents.

A friend had asked him to go to a home for elderly people on Christmas Day and play the piano—George Mason was a good musician. But he had made some excuse or other; he had intended to sit at home with a good cigar, listening to some new recordings he was giving himself.

George Mason dug his nails into the palms of his hands until the pain balanced the misery in his mind. Nobody would come and let him out. Nobody, nobody...

Miserably the whole of Christmas Day went by, and the succeeding night.

On the morning after Christmas the head clerk came into the office at the usual time, opened the safe, then went on into his private office. No one saw George Mason stagger out into the corridor, run to the water cooler, and drink great gulps of water. No one paid any attention to him as he left and took a taxi home.

There he shaved, changed his wrinkled clothes, ate breakfast, and returned to his office, where his employees greeted him casually.

That day he met several acquaintances and talked to his own brother. Grimly, inexorably, the truth closed in on George Mason. He had vanished from human society during the great festival of brotherhood; no one had missed him at all.

Reluctantly, George Mason began to think about the true meaning of Christmas. Was it possible that he had been blind all these years with selfishness, indifference, pride? Wasn't giving, after all, the essence of Christmas because it marked the time God gave His own Son to the world?

All through the year that followed, with little, hesitant deeds of kindness, with small, unnoticed acts of unselfishness, George Mason tried to prepare himself....

Now, once more, it was Christmas Eve.

Slowly he backed out of the safe, closed it. He touched its grim steel face lightly, almost affectionately, and left the office.

There he goes now in his black overcoat and hat, the same George Mason as a year ago. Or is it? He walks a few blocks, then flags a taxi, anxious not to be late. His nephews are expecting him to help them trim the tree. Afterwards, he is taking his brother and his sister-in-law to a Christmas play.

Why is he so happy? Why does this jostling against others, laden as he is with bundles, exhilarate and delight him?

Perhaps the card has something to do with it, the card he taped inside his office safe last New Year's Day. On the card is written, in George Mason's own hand: "To love people, to be indispensable somewhere, that is the purpose of life. That is the secret of happiness."

ECK THE HALLS

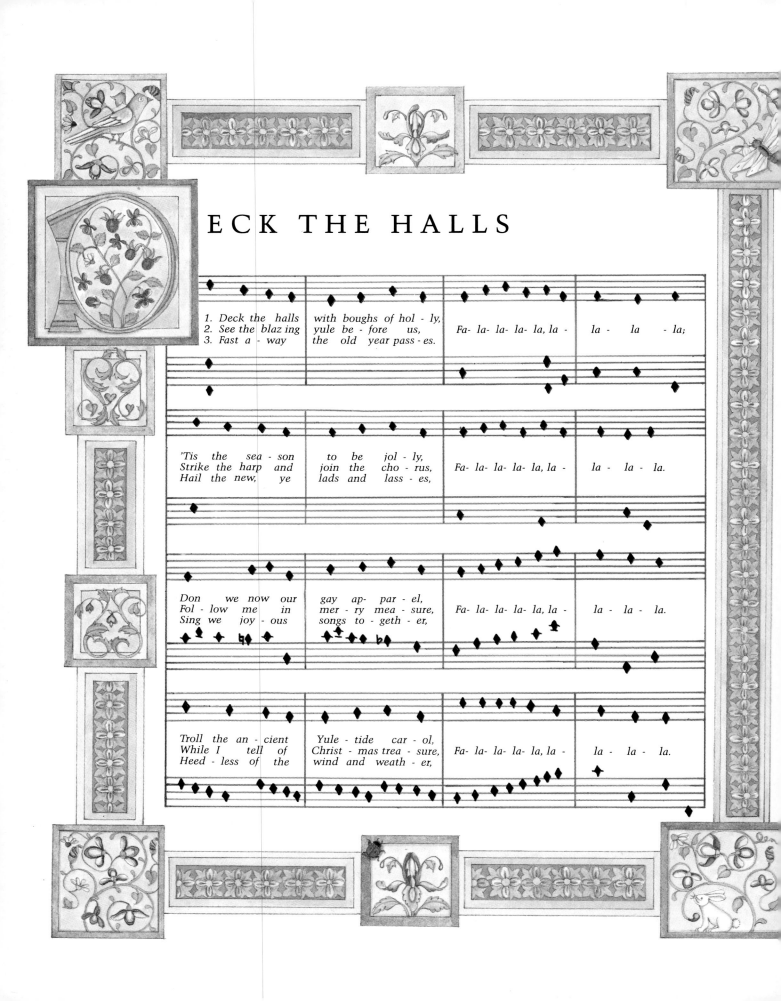

1. Deck the halls with boughs of hol - ly, Fa- la- la- la- la, la- la - la - la;
2. See the blaz ing yule be - fore us,
3. Fast a - way the old year pass - es.

'Tis the sea - son to be jol - ly, Fa- la- la- la- la, la- la - la - la.
Strike the harp and join the cho - rus,
Hail the new, ye lads and lass - es,

Don we now our gay ap- par- el, Fa- la- la- la- la, la- la - la - la.
Fol - low me in mer - ry mea - sure,
Sing we joy - ous songs to - geth - er,

Troll the an - cient Yule - tide car - ol, Fa- la- la- la- la, la- la - la - la.
While I tell of Christ - mas trea - sure,
Heed - less of the wind and weath - er,

CHAPTER

THE WONDER OF
CHRISTMAS AND
CHILDREN

THE FIRST NOEL

Have you ever wondered about the origin of the word *noel*? We sing it in carols and see it on Christmas cards, but what does it mean?

The origin goes back to the French word for "birth." There are several explanations about its Christmas usage, but the one I like the best goes back to medieval England. It was common then to abbreviate a common phrase into one word in order to save time; for example, the phrase *God be with you* gradually became *good-bye*. During Christmas, it seems people cried out a greeting to one another as they passed in the streets. "Now all is well," they shouted, referring to the event of God sending His Son. The theory goes that with time the phrase was contracted into one word, *noel*.

Today I cannot sing the word or read it upon a card without its full meaning filling me with new peace. Christ is born into our darkness. *Now all is well!*

Sue Monk Kidd

THE FIRST CAROL

Did you ever wonder why Christmas songs are called carols? The word *carol* means "circle dance." Long ago, caroling was common at village festivals. People would dance arm-in-arm, singing happy songs with simple, beautiful melodies. Carols became one of the ways Christians expressed their joy at Christmas.

Because he encouraged the singing of Christmas carols, St. Francis of Assisi is sometimes called the Father of the Christmas Carol.

Mary Lou Carney

CHRISTMAS POEMS

O Lord Jesus, who for love of us
lay as a baby in the manger,
we thank You that by Your coming
You brought joy to all the world.
Help us at this glad time
to try to make others happy for Your sake.

Jesus Christ, Thou child so wise,
Bless mine hands and fill mine eyes,
And bring my soul to Paradise.

Thank You, God, for the joys of Christmas:
for the fun of opening Christmas stockings;
for Christmas trees with sparkling lights;
for exciting parties; for Christmas cakes and puddings;
thank You, God.
Thank You for all the happiness of Christmas-time;
thank You for all the lovely presents we receive;
thank You most of all that Jesus was born
as a baby on the first Christmas Day.
Thank You, God.

Grant, heavenly Father,
that as we keep the birthday of Jesus,
He may be born again in our hearts,
and that we may grow in the likeness
of the Son of God,
who for our sake was born Son of Man.

THE FRIENDLY BEASTS

Jesus our brother, strong and good,
Was humbly born in a stable rude,
And the friendly beasts around Him stood,
Jesus our brother, strong and good.

"I," said the donkey, shaggy and brown,
"I carried His mother up hill and down,
I carried her safely to Bethlehem town;
I," said the donkey, shaggy and brown.

"I," said the cow, all white and red,
"I gave Him my manger for His bed,
I gave Him my hay to pillow His head;
I," said the cow, all white and red.

"I," said the sheep, with curly horn,
"I gave Him my wool for His blanket warm,
He wore my coat on Christmas morn;
I," said the sheep, with curly horn.

"I," said the dove, from the rafters high,
"Cooed Him to sleep, my mate and I,
We cooed Him to sleep, my mate and I;
I," said the dove, from the rafters high.

And every beast, by some good spell,
In the stable dark was glad to tell,
Of the gift he gave Immanuel,
The gift he gave Immanuel.

CHRISTMAS GREETINGS FROM A FAIRY TO A CHILD

Lady dear, if Fairies may
For a moment lay aside
Cunning tricks and elfish play,
'Tis at happy Christmas-tide.

We have heard the children say—
Gentle children, whom we love—
Long ago, on Christmas Day,
Came a message from above.

Still, as Christmas-tide comes round,
They remember it again—
Echo still the joyful sound,
"Peace on earth, good-will to men."

Yet the hearts must child-like be
Where such heavenly guests abide,
Unto children, in their glee,
All the year is Christmas-tide.

Thus, forgetting tricks and play
For a moment, Lady dear,
We would wish you, if we may,
Merry Christmas, glad New Year.

Christmas, 1887
Lewis Carroll

HOLLY AND TINSEL

Holly and tinsel and
shiny bright balls,
Pageant rehearsals
and trips to the mall.
Singing old carols
in soft candlelight,
Knowing the Christ Child
was born on this night.
Sweet giggled secrets
that no one can hear—
All these make Christmas
the *best* time of year!

Mary Lou Carney

TO A CHRISTMAS
TWO-YEAR-OLD

Child, and all children,
come and celebrate
the little one who came,
threatened by hate
and Herod's sword.
Sing softly and rejoice
in the reward
for all the baby boys
of Bethlehem
who died
in Jesus' place.
Small wonder when He grew
He wanted children by His side,
stretched out His arms, stood,
beckoned you,
called *Come to me*
and died
in your place
so that you could.

Luci Shaw

CRADLE HYMN

Away in a manger, no crib for a bed,
The little Lord Jesus laid down His
sweet head.
The stars in the bright sky looked down
where He lay—
The little Lord Jesus, asleep on the hay.

Martin Luther

WHY CHRISTMAS TREES AREN'T PERFECT

Richard H. Schneider

They say that if you creep into an evergreen forest late at night you can hear the trees talking. If you listen very carefully to the whisper of the wind, you can hear the older pines telling the younger ones why they will never be perfect. They will always have a bent branch here, a gap there. . . .

But long, long ago all evergreen trees *were* perfect. Each one took special pride in branches that sloped smoothly down from pointed top to evenly shaped skirt.

This was especially true in a small kingdom far beyond the Carpathian Mountains in Europe. Here the evergreen trees were the most beautiful of all. For here the sun shone just right, not too hot, not too dim. Here the rain fell just enough to keep the ground moist and soft so no tree went thirsty. And here the snow fell gently day after day to keep every branch fresh and green.

Each year as Christmas approached, the Queen's woodsmen would search the royal evergreen forest for the most perfect, most beautiful tree. The one fortunate enough to be chosen would be cut on the first Saturday of Advent. It would then be carefully carried to the castle and set up in the center of the great hall. There it reigned in honor for all the Christmas celebrations.

Out in the hushed forest every evergreen hoped for this honor. Each tree tried to grow its branches and needles to perfection. All of them strained to have the best form and appearance.

One tree, Small Pine, grew near the edge of the forest and promised to be the most beautiful of all. As a seedling it had listened carefully to the older trees who knew what was best for young saplings. And it had tried so very hard to grow just right. As a result, everything about Small Pine, from its deep sea-green color to the curling tip of its evenly spaced branches, was perfect.

It had, in fact, already overheard jealous whispers from the other trees. But it paid them no mind. Small Pine knew that if one did one's very best, what anyone else said didn't matter.

One cold night, when a bright full moon glittered on the crusty snow, a little gray rabbit came hopping as fast as he could into the grove of evergreens. The rabbit's furry sides heaved in panic. From beyond the hill came the howling of wild dogs in the thrill of the hunt. The bunny, his eyes wide with fright, frantically searched for cover. But the dark, cold trees lifted their branches artfully from the snow and frowned. They did not like this interruption of their quiet evening when growing was at its best.

Faster and faster the rabbit circled as the excited howling of the dogs sounded louder and louder.

And then Small Pine's heart shuddered. When the terrified rabbit ran near, Small Pine dipped its lower branches down, down, down to the snow. And in that instant before the wild dogs broke into the grove, the rabbit slipped under Small Pine's evergreen screen. He huddled safely among the comforting branches while the dogs galloped by and disappeared into the forest.

In the morning the rabbit went home to his

burrow, and Small Pine tried to lift its lower branches back up to their proper height. It strained and struggled, but the branches had been pressed down too long through the night. *Oh well*, Small Pine thought, *no matter*. Perhaps the woodsmen wouldn't notice a few uneven branches near the ground in a tree so beautiful.

Several days later a terrible blizzard lashed the land. No one remembered ever having so much wind and snow. Villagers slammed their shutters tight while birds and animals huddled in their nests and dens.

A brown mother wren had become lost in the
storm. With feathers so wet she could barely fly, she
went from one large evergreen to another looking for
a shelter. But each tree she approached feared the
wren would ruin its perfect shape and clenched its
branches tight, like a fist.

Finally, the exhausted wren fluttered toward
Small Pine. Once more Small Pine's heart opened
and so did its branches. The mother wren nestled on

a branch near the top, secure at last. But when the storm ended and the bird had flown away, Small Pine could not move its top branches back into their perfect shape.

In them would be a gap evermore.

Days passed and winter deepened. The packed snow had frozen so hard that the deer in the forest could not reach the tender ground moss, which they ate to survive. Only the older, stronger deer could dig through the icy snow with their hooves.

One little fawn had wandered away from his mother. Now he was starving. He inched into the pine grove and noticed the soft, tender evergreen tips. He tried to nibble on them, but every tree quickly withdrew its needles so the tiny deer teeth couldn't chew them.

Thin and weak, he staggered against Small Pine. Pity filled the tree's heart, and it stretched out its soft needles for the starving fawn to eat. But alas, when the deer was strong enough to scamper away, Small Pine's branches looked very ragged.

Small Pine wilted in sorrow. It could hear what the larger, still-perfect trees were saying about how bad it looked. A tear of pine gum oozed from the tip of a branch. Small Pine knew it could never hope for the honor of being the Queen's Christmas tree.

Lost in despair, Small Pine did not see the good Queen come with the woodsmen into the forest. It was the first Saturday of Advent, and she had come to choose the finest tree herself because this was a special celebration year in the history of her kingdom.

As the royal sleigh, drawn by two white horses, slowly passed through the forest, her careful eye scanned the evergreens. Each one was hoping to be the royal choice.

When the Queen saw Small Pine, a flush of anger filled her. How could such an ugly tree with so many drooping branches and gaps be allowed in the royal forest? She decided to have a woodsman cut it to throw away and nodded for the sleigh to drive on.

But then . . . she raised her hand for the sleigh to stop and glanced back at the forlorn little pine.

She noticed the tracks of small animals under its uneven needles. She saw a wren's feather caught in its branches. And, as she studied the gaping hole in its side and its ragged shape, understanding filled her heart.

"This is the one," she said, and pointed to Small Pine. The woodsmen gasped, but they did as the Queen directed.

To the astonishment of all the evergreens in the forest, Small Pine was carried away to the great hall in the castle. There it was decorated with shimmering, silver stars and golden angels, which sparkled and flashed in the light of thousands of glowing candles.

On Christmas Day a huge Yule log blazed in the fireplace at the end of the great hall. While orange

flames chuckled and crackled, the Queen's family and all the villagers danced and sang together around Small Pine. And everyone who danced and sang around it said that Small Pine was the finest Christmas tree yet. For in looking at its drooping, nibbled branches, they saw the protecting arm of their father or the comforting lap of a mother. And some, like the wise Queen, saw the love of Christ expressed on earth.

So if you walk among evergreens today, you will find, along with rabbits, birds, and other happy living things, many trees like Small Pine. You will see a drooping limb, which gives cover, a gap offering a warm resting place, or branches ragged from feeding hungry animals.

For, as have many of us, the trees have learned that living for the sake of others makes us most beautiful in the eyes of God.

THE STABLE CAT

I'm a Stable Cat, a working cat,
I clear the place of vermin.
The cat at the inn
    is never thin
But I am never fat.

But I don't complain of that—
I'm lithe and sleek and clever.
The mice I chase
    about the place,
For I'm the Stable Cat.

But tonight, well, things are different.
I make the small mice welcome.
I ask them all
    to pay a call
And keep my claws in velvet.

Sparrows out of the weather,
The mild, roo-cooing pigeons,
These flying bands
    are all my friends.
We're happy together.

All live things under this roof,
All birds, beasts, and insects,
We look with joy
    at Mary's boy,
Are safe in His love.

Leslie Norris

CHRISTMAS FUN STUFF

H ere's your chance to write and design an original, one-of-a-kind Christmas card for someone special. Ready?

Don't you love sorting through cookbooks for fudge cookies or yummy candy recipes? But did you know that poems can have "recipes," too? Here is a "recipe" for a four-line Christmas poem:

Line 1 Three words that describe Christmas
Line 2 Two "ing" words
Line 3 Sentence or group of words
Line 4 Christmas greeting

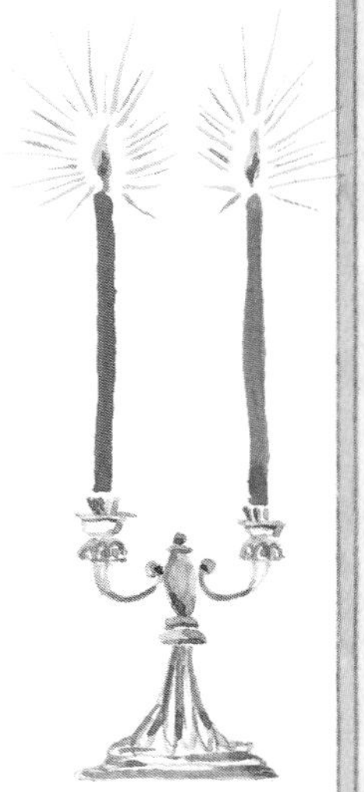

It's easier than it looks! (And you can't burn it or put in too much sugar or forget to stir it.) Here's a sample to show you how:

CHRISTMAS
Busy, bright, fun
Sparkling, bustling
My favorite time of year
Happy Holidays!

Now try your own four-line poem on the lines below. Use the "recipe" above, or create your own.

Copy your poem on paper, illustrate it with your homemade Christmas borders or cut-out pictures, and mail (or hand deliver) this custom-made card to a special friend or relative.

Mary Lou Carney

S C R A F T S

CHRISTMAS FINGERPRINTS

You can—you *do*—own your own private "printing" press!

This year why don't you design your own original greeting cards for the holidays? They will be different from anybody else's because no two sets of fingerprints are exactly the same. And that is what you will be using.

First, choose any kind of white or colored paper you wish to use. You will also need a felt-tip pen and an ink pad. And, of course, your nonidentical printing press.

Just place your thumb or finger on the ink pad—hard. Then press the inked finger on the paper, rolling just a little from left to right. Continue adding prints until you have created a design—a Christmas Tree, a cross, an animal, a star, a shepherd—there's no end to the holiday pictures you can create with your fingerprints.

Use the felt-tip pen to outline your design and add such touches as a crook for the shepherd, lights on the Christmas tree, streams of light from the star. Let your imagination run wild. Your family and friends will know immediately they are receiving something very special this Christmas.

June Masters Bacher

MAKE YOUR OWN CHRISTMAS GIFT WRAP

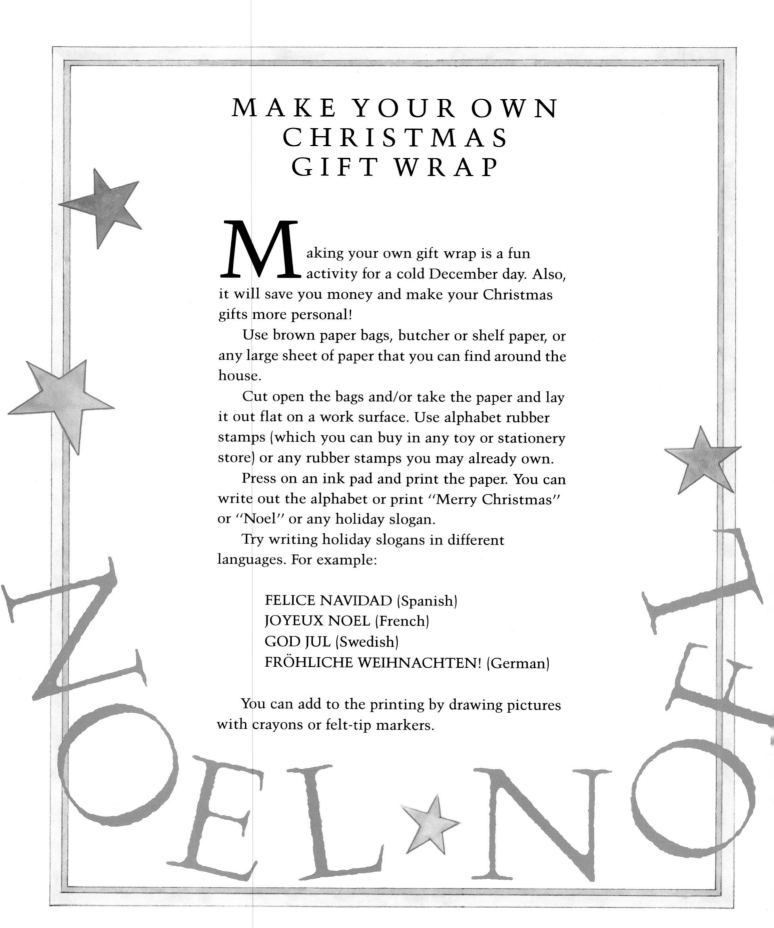

Making your own gift wrap is a fun activity for a cold December day. Also, it will save you money and make your Christmas gifts more personal!

Use brown paper bags, butcher or shelf paper, or any large sheet of paper that you can find around the house.

Cut open the bags and/or take the paper and lay it out flat on a work surface. Use alphabet rubber stamps (which you can buy in any toy or stationery store) or any rubber stamps you may already own.

Press on an ink pad and print the paper. You can write out the alphabet or print "Merry Christmas" or "Noel" or any holiday slogan.

Try writing holiday slogans in different languages. For example:

FELICE NAVIDAD (Spanish)
JOYEUX NOEL (French)
GOD JUL (Swedish)
FRÖHLICHE WEIHNACHTEN! (German)

You can add to the printing by drawing pictures with crayons or felt-tip markers.

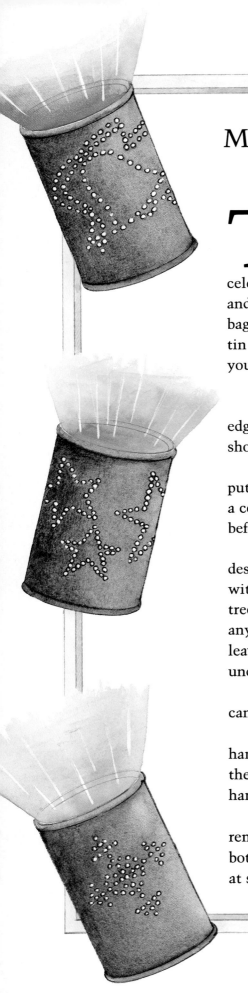

MAKE "LIGHT" AT CHRISTMAS

These special holiday punched-tin candles add a warm glow to any holiday celebration and make lovely gifts for your family and friends. If you've made luminarias out of paper bags and sand, you'll really enjoy forging them from tin cans. With these instructions, you can create your own designs.

You'll need plain tin cans with all the rough edges pinched flat and smoothed out. (Mom or Dad should help out with this project!)

Fill the cans with water and freeze them by putting in the freezer or leaving outside if you live in a cold climate. (The water needs to be frozen solid before removing from the cold.)

Use a permanent felt-tip ink marker to draw a design on the outside of the can. Make your design with little dots. You can draw a Christmas star, a tree, your name, an animal, a holiday symbol, or anything else that comes to mind. Make sure to leave at least one inch from the bottom of the can undecorated.

Lay a bath towel on a flat surface, and place the can on its side.

Position a nail at the first dot, and carefully hammer it through the tin. (The ice will prevent the nail from bending.) In this way, continue hammering until you have completed your drawing.

Allow the ice to melt and pour out the water that remains in the can. Place a votive candle in the bottom of the can. Put your luminaria outside, and at sunset, ask an adult to light the candle for you.

FUN WITH PAPER GINGERBREAD GARLAND

Paper Gingerbread People are fun to make—even though you can't eat them!

Take two large brown paper grocery bags and cut them to lay flat. Use a cookie cutter in the shape of a gingerbread man (or make your own from cardboard) and trace the pattern on the brown paper.

Use scissors to cut out each gingerbread man. Decorate each one with art supplies such as crayons or felt-tip markers, glue, glitter, and bits of string or fabric.

You string together a group of your decorated gingerbread men by attaching them to a three-foot ribbon. (Attach to the ribbon with glue or cut a small hole at the top of each man and tie on with a small piece of yarn or string.)

Hang them on your tree, your door, on the mantel place, or anywhere in your house that needs a touch of holiday cheer!

CREATE A FESTIVE DOOR

You can bring the holidays to your very own room by creating a huge Christmas ornament out of your door. Ask one of your parents for permission and then let your creativity run wild!

First, you will need a very large piece of art or brown butcher paper that is the same size as your bedroom door. (If you can't find one big piece, then tape together several smaller pieces. You can also use brown paper bags, cut apart and stretched out flat.)

You'll need a big flat surface to work on. Lay out the paper. If you share a room with a brother or sister, ask Mom to divide the paper into even sections so that each of you has a separate space in which to work. Or, you can work together with your sibling to create one special design.

Gather together all of your art supplies: crayons, felt-tip markers, glue or tape, scissors, glitter, notepads, stickers, construction paper. Ask Mom for scraps of fabric or string. Perhaps your parents have some old magazines that you can cut up to make a collage of letters and pictures. You may also want to add some photographs of family, friends, or pets.

Using all of these materials (and your own imagination!), make a colorful Christmas picture.

Here are some suggestions:
    ** a Christmas tree with lots of gift packages;
    ** a "Winter Wonderland" scene of your favorite Christmas-time activities such as skating, skiing, or sledding; or
    ** scenes from a favorite Christmas story.

As the season progresses, you can add to your design by taping on favorite Christmas cards or special photos of friends and family.

When your project is completed and all the glue has dried, hang the paper on your door with masking tape or small nails. (Mom or Dad should help with the nails.) A string of mini-Christmas-lights will make your holiday door even more festive!

HE TWELVE DAYS OF CHRISTMAS

1. On the first day of Christ mas my true love sent to me A

par - tridge __ in a pear tree.

2. On the se – cond
3. On the third __ day of Christ – mas my true love sent to me
4. On the fourth __

Two tur - tle doves
Three French hens, (two etc.) and a par - tridge in a pear tree.
Four call- ing birds, (three etc.)

(Repeat as necessary)

CHAPTER VI

FAMILY TRADITIONS AND HOMEMADE GIVING

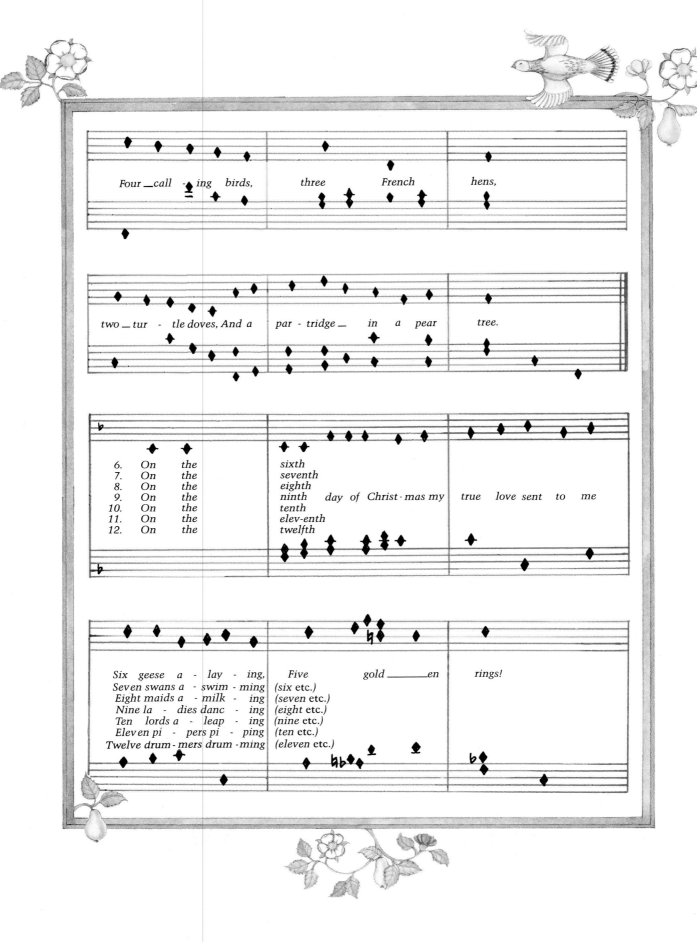

THE FAMILIAR CHRISTMAS GIFT

Sue Monk Kidd

One December when my daughter Ann was only six, she tucked two gifts beneath the Christmas tree, one for her daddy, the other for me. "What do you suppose they are?" I asked my husband. He shrugged, as puzzled as I.

On Christmas morning I opened my gift to find a pair of slightly familiar-looking silver earrings. In her daddy's package was a navy tie with little tan ducks on it.

"Why, Ann," I exclaimed, genuinely amazed. "Where did you get these lovely gifts?"

"The old chest," she answered.

That's when I recognized the earrings as some I'd retired to the chest at least ten years before. The tie had been discarded long ago, too. Ann had given us gifts we already possessed!

And she had reminded me of something important. Christmas should not be simply the experience of getting more, but waking up to what we already possess. For God has already given us everything we need: a Savior, love, hope, eternal life, beauty, peace of mind, joy, faith, community . . . so much. Only we don't always experience them. With time and familiarity we tend to lose touch with God's abundance.

So this Christmas let's not just open what is new beneath the tree, but *re*open what is already ours!

A CHRISTMAS FAMILY CALENDAR

Carol Kuykendall

The presents you make are always the best!" I've repeatedly told our three children since their preschool days. Our home is filled with a priceless collection of papier-mâché objects, lumpy clay ashtrays, collages of family pictures, and framed Scripture verses with illustrations.

A few years ago, we came up with a "present-you-can-make" idea for grandparents, which my husband Lynn's parents now claim is their favorite Christmas present. It's our own personalized, wall-hanging calendar, which is as much fun to make as it is to receive. Gather together lots of heavy, colored construction paper, a hole-puncher, scissors, glue, some yarn, a picture-calendar that comes in the mail this time of year, and a pile of family photos you're willing to give away.

We copy the format of any wall-hanging calendar. First, we cut the pages of the month off the new picture calendar, paste them on separate sheets of construction paper, and make a collage of pictures and artwork to go with that month. We add a few captions, Scripture verses, or monthly reminders and tie the whole thing together with colorful yarn. Each child does his or her birthday month, and we divide up the rest of the pages. The result is a photo-summary of a year in the life of our family, which, according to our Mamma and Pappa, blesses them from their kitchen wall every single day of the year.

Why don't you create your own family-photo calendar for some faraway relative or friend this Christmas?

LIGHTING THE CANDLES OF ADVENT

Terry Helwig

Tomorrow is Advent. And as I sit in my favorite chair and watch the evening shadows creep into the family room, I think about the Advent candle-lighting service at our church that our family will be part of this season. Yet in my solitude this evening, I wish for a more *personal* celebration of Advent—one between just God and me. I long to discover a more private meaning of Christmas, one that will satisfy an inner desire to draw close to Him this Holy Season.

Suddenly I perk up. "Why not create my own *personal* Advent wreath?" Not too formal; one that wouldn't look out of place amid the clutter of books and papers on the table next to my "quiet" chair in the family room. Excitedly, I begin my search for a handmade Advent wreath. In a kitchen drawer, I discover five birthday candles left over from my daughter Mandy's sixth birthday. In a cabinet, I find a round, metal band of a Mason jar lid from the applesauce I canned last fall. I turn the tarnished band upside down and secure the candles in a circle to the inside rim with melted wax. A sprig of holly from the dining table centerpiece, and my makeshift wreath is complete. No, my little crown of leaning candles does not resemble the traditional Advent wreath, but I rather like it.

I'm ready to begin. Each Sunday of Advent I'll set aside a private moment when I can retreat to the family room and light my tiny candles of Advent. Perhaps these Christmas flames will bring to life within me a deeper love for God and others. Or release me from pride by bringing me understanding. Or help me to let go of a long-held grudge through the light of forgiveness.

Perhaps, this Advent, I can keep the Light of God's love burning all 365 days of the new year.

A BRIGHT, ORANGE CHRISTMAS

Marilyn Moore Jensen

I was feeling blue about how Christmas had changed. Mother was in a nursing home in Wisconsin, my children were grown and living away from home, I was alone in Connecticut. There would be no stockings hung, no oranges in the toes—a tradition in our family from my mother's childhood on a farm. On Christmas Eve there, neighboring farm families would gather at the old Zion Church. After carols, recitations, and Bible readings, one of the farmers, dressed as Santa Claus, would give each child a gift—an orange. Before the age of air transport and refrigeration, fresh oranges were a delicacy, especially at Christmastime, when their golden glow must have seemed like a light of hope to those Welsh immigrants struggling through a hard Wisconsin winter.

After Mother married my father, she continued the custom, and my sisters, brother, and I always found oranges in the toes of our Christmas stockings. Somehow Mother kept alive the Christmas wonder of her childhood. Later, I would put oranges in my own children's stockings. But now what would happen to the tradition?

Then when I received the crate of oranges my friend had sent from Florida I got the new idea . . .

For three days and nights I worked on the oranges, slicing them and boiling them with sugar. I sterilized glasses, and the steam filled the house and billowed out into the cold winter air. Finally, there, lined up on the windowsill, were gleaming glasses filled with marmalade. New gifts and a new tradition! Here was one for Mother . . . there's some for the neighbors . . . these will be for the children . . . *oh, merry, merry Christmas*!

If you're feeling blue about some changes this Christmas, maybe you need to find something new to hold your wonder. You've heard the saying: turn lemons into lemonade. *Or, oranges into marmalade!*

AN ANGEL SONG
AT CHRISTMAS

Carol Knapp

When I was growing up, I loved Christmas Eve, because it was the night Mom would sing "Sweet Little Jesus Boy" at our candle-lighting church service. Her pure soprano voice cradled each note, making the song a prayer that reached shadowed corners of church and hearts alike. I'd sit entranced, thinking that's how an angel must sound.

After I was married, with children of my own, I still loved hearing Mom's "Sweet Little Jesus Boy" every Christmas. One year, on a whim, I asked if I could tape-record her. She paused on her way out my door, wearing a bright red scarf over her white hair, and began to sing.

The very next year found us thousands of miles apart. My family had moved to the woods of Alaska. It was Christmas Eve. A lonely time when you're in a new place far from "home." I remembered the tape recording I had made and quietly slipped outside and crunched up and down the frozen drive playing "Sweet Little Jesus Boy" over and over. Mom's voice hung in the clear night air like an angel song. Not even the frigid temperature could keep my loneliness from melting away. I looked up at the stars . . . and God, and whispered, "Merry Christmas!"

SHARING CHRISTMAS
WITH OTHERS

Phyllis Hobe

What do you do when you're alone at Christmas? Hope you'll be invited out to dinner? Sit by yourself, remembering how good it felt to have a family around you? Take a trip to get away from your loneliness? Perhaps you think that hospitality has no place in your life any more. Well, if you do, then you're mistaken. Over a third of the adult population in the United States lives alone—and Christmas is for them, too.

Jesus was alone. But there was hospitality in His heart. He didn't wait to be invited somewhere; He invited friends— and strangers—to be with Him. He didn't have a home as we know it, yet He welcomed people into His life. And they brought Him joy.

My friend Peggy Bates tells me that after she had been widowed for two years, she decided it was time to stop shutting Christmas out of her life. "So I told my children and my grandchildren and all the aunts and uncles that that year I wanted them to come to my house. It was a lot of work, and I cried at times because it brought back memories of my husband. But we all had such a happy Christmas that I've been doing the same thing every year. It brings me back into life!"

Yes, hospitality can do that. So, if you don't want to be alone this Christmas, open your home, your heart, and your life to the people you know.

BABY JESUS AND THE BREAD BOX

Patricia Lorenz

The week before Advent, I asked nine-year-old Andrew to set up the manger scene on the chest in the entryway of our home. He carefully unwrapped the delicate, hand-painted animals, shepherds, wise men, Mary, Joseph and placed the Baby Jesus in the wooden manger. The next day, I noticed Baby Jesus was missing. *Andrew's playing a joke on me*, I thought.

Later, when I started fixing supper, I opened the bread box on the kitchen counter, and there was Baby Jesus next to the bread! When I asked Andrew about this, his explanation was simple. "In religion class, Mrs. Hatzenbeller said Jesus is the bread of life, Mom. Besides, He shouldn't be in the manger until Christmas."

Ever since Andrew put Jesus in the bread box, it has become a family tradition. Now, from the first day of Advent until Christmas Eve, Jesus sits on top of or in the bread box to remind us that He is the bread of life. Each time I reach for the bread, I'm reminded to say a quick prayer of thanksgiving for our daily blessings, including our daily bread. On Christmas Eve, almost ceremoniously, Andrew places the baby in the manger between Mary and Joseph.

After the Epiphany, we put the manger scene away for the year. All except for Baby Jesus; He goes back in the bread box as a daily reminder that, just like our daily bread, the spirit of Christmas is an everyday, year-long event.

AFTER-CHRISTMAS SURPRISE

Carol Kuykendall

In the early-morning darkness of our cold, quiet house, I wrap myself up in an old terry robe, pour a mug of hot coffee, plug in the Christmas tree lights, and settle down on the couch to appreciate Christmas alone with God. I haven't missed a morning since we put up the tree, but today something is undeniably different . . . Christmas is over. Like a little kid, I feel strangely forlorn. Instead of exciting preparations, today I face only the obligation of cleaning up and writing thank-you notes. I sigh, thinking back over the season's most precious moments: the magnificent Christmas music at church; the annual neighborhood party where three generations of families joined together to read the Christmas story; the sight of our spunky, eighty-year-old Mawma and Pawpa driving into our yard early Christmas morning, in spite of the predicted snowstorm. I am thankful for all these memories.

Thankful . . . aha! Instead of only the expected "thank yous" for *things* received, how about some unexpected thank-you notes to the memory-makers of the year past? As I start to make a mental list, I realize the task might take several days, but the thought of surprising people with unexpected notes zips the Christmas spirit right back into my morning.

Who was responsible for some of the giggles and goose bumps of *your* year? Why not surprise them with unexpected notes?

OOD
KING WENCESLAS

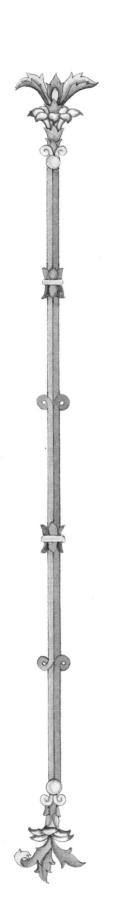

CHAPTER

FAMILY CHRISTMAS MEALS AND RECIPES

CHRISTMAS DAY
BREAKFAST RECIPES
GRANDPA'S FAMILY FARM CHRISTMAS

Phyllis Walk

Grandpa used to get real "het up" whenever we'd have a family Christmas on the farm. He was an early riser and expected everyone else to be the same. He wanted breakfast promptly at 6 a.m. so he could do chores before we had prayers and opened presents.

Late one Christmas Eve, Grandma gathered all the children and seventeen grandchildren to announce: "Anyone who wants to help Grandpa feed the calves and chickens, gather the eggs, and see the baby colt better be up at 6 a.m. Dress warm and plan on having 'Glug-in-a-mug' and an oat scone with Grandpa."

"Grandma, what's that glug-stuff-in-a-mug?" everyone wanted to know.

"Be up at 6 a.m. and you'll find out," she said with a pert nod of her head.

It worked like a charm. Next morning, ten grandchildren and four of their mothers and dads were up at 6 a.m. to have scones and "glug." Then everyone went to help with the chores.

Every year saw another three or four added to the list of helpers, and finally, the year before Grandpa left the farm, everyone participated. It made him "happy as a pig-in-a-mudhole" to have all the family pitch in.

Though there isn't a farm left in the family, as soon as all the kids are married and our family grows, I plan to adopt Grandpa and Grandma Foster's early-morning tradition when everyone comes home for the holidays.

Glug-in-a-Mug

Here is Grandma's recipe modified a little, using more modern products and utensils than she had.

1 package instant oatmeal
2 cups hot milk
1 T. honey
**   cinnamon or nutmeg**
**   banana or other fruit desired**

Put instant oatmeal, either plain or spiced, in a blender. Add hot milk and honey heated until runny. Whirl to mix well and serve with a dusting of cinnamon or nutmeg. Half a banana or a piece or two of canned fruit may be added for variety from time to time if desired. This serves 1 person, but several servings can be made at once.

Scottish Oat Scones

Combine the following dry ingredients and mix well:

1½ cups flour
1¼ cups quick oats
¼   cup sugar
1   T. baking powder
1   tsp. cream of tartar
½   tsp. salt

Add:

⅔   cup melted butter or margarine
⅓   cup milk

Mix until dry ingredients are moistened. Then stir in:

1   cup raisins or currants

Shape dough to form a ball. It will be slightly moist and sticky. Pat out on a lightly floured surface to form an 8-inch circle. Cut into 8 to 12 wedges and, using a spatula, lift onto a greased cookie sheet, placing wedges slightly apart. Bake at 425° F. until golden brown—usually 12 to 15 minutes. Serve warm with

honey, butter, or old-fashioned preserves. (Dough may also be frozen successfully after it has been cut in wedges by placing waxed paper between slices and wrapping in plastic. Just remove from freezer and let thaw 10 minutes or more before baking.)

Bismarcks
Mickey Campbell Davis

Shortly after the turn of the century, in a cottage in the Black Forest region in Germany, my stepfather, as a young boy, took his turn grinding fresh coffee beans for breakfast, while another of the children went to the village bake shop for fresh sweet rolls hot from the ovens. When his turn came to get the rolls, he ran as fast as his little legs would carry him through the dark and menacing woods. I asked what kinds of rolls he got. His face alight, he told me, "All kinds, but me favorite was den Bismarcks." He remembered them made of yeast dough, spiced, big as his fist, dark brown, and covered with sugar.

1 cup scalded milk
¼ yeast cake, dissolved
¼ cup water, lukewarm
1 tsp. salt
⅓ cup butter
1 cup brown sugar
2 eggs, well beaten
½ tsp. grated nutmeg
2 cups flour
**   granulated sugar**

Cool milk to lukewarm, add yeast cake in water, salt, and flour, enough to make stiff batter. Add melted butter, brown sugar, eggs, nutmeg. You may also add cinnamon if you like. Add rest of flour and more, if needed, until batter is very stiff. Let rise, covered with damp cloth, until double in bulk. Punch down, turn onto floured board, roll 3/4-inch thick.

Cut out with biscuit cutter and roll into balls. Place on floured board or cloth and let rise 1 hour. Turn and let rise again. Fry in oil at an even temperature of 370° F. until brown, turn carefully and brown on other side. Remove carefully, drain on crumpled brown paper. When almost cool, roll in granulated sugar. Makes about 2 dozen.

AN OHIO CHRISTMAS BREAKFAST

Judy Rogers

Early Christmas morning, arising without eating, my father and I would feed the wild birds and rabbits by sweeping a spot in the snow in the vacant lot beside our house. Sometimes we would load our black station wagon with carrots, suet, celery, straw, and other edibles. We would find an unspoiled spot near our home, shovel the snow if necessary, and put out a Christmas feast for the deer, rabbits, squirrels, opossums, and birds. After watching a while, we would return home to a large breakfast my mother had prepared.

Mother believed in making an unbroken circle on Christmas morning: once we were all seated, joined hands, and said a prayer, no one rose, no matter what might have been forgotten. Our traditional breakfast menu:

Grit
•
French Toast
•
Bacon
•
Hot Chocolate
•
Orange Juice

Grit

The recipe for the Grit, or Vanilla Pudding, is a standard one, found on cornstarch boxes, with two exceptions: add 2 beaten egg yolks while cooking, and use fresh cinnamon.

Combine in a small saucepan:
3 T. cornstarch
½ tsp. salt
⅓ cup sugar
Gradually add:
2 cups milk
2 egg yolks, beaten

Boil gently, stirring constantly. Add and stir in 1 tsp. vanilla just before serving. Pour into 4 small dessert cups. For large appetites or more than 4 people, double recipe. Dust with freshly grated or ground cinnamon.

French Toast

1 loaf bread
2 cups milk
2 eggs, beaten
1 tsp. vanilla
1 T. sugar
2 T. shortening or butter
**   powdered sugar**
**   maple syrup**

Use an uncut loaf of "stuffing," or bakery bread, sliced 1-inch thick. In a 13x9x2-inch pan place bread slices flat. Mix well milk, eggs, vanilla, sugar. Pour mixture over bread in pan and place in refrigerator overnight. Bread will absorb liquid. In skillet over medium heat melt shortening or butter (add more as necessary). When hot, add the saturated bread slices carefully. Brown and turn. Sprinkle with powdered sugar and serve with real maple syrup. If cooking for a crowd, double or triple as needed. Bread can be dipped instead of soaking all night, but I do like the soaked bread better.

CHRISTMAS DINNER

GRAMPA MORGAN'S CHRISTMAS DINNER

Oscar Greene

For weeks I struggled to remember what made up those delicious Christmas dinners at Grampa Morgan's that I enjoyed as a child. They went back to the year 1927. Then, Aunt Ruth, 81, came to my rescue by reciting the menu from memory.

I remember Grampa standing at the head of our dining room table, leading eighteen to twenty of us in prayer. We joined hearts and thanked God for blessings received during the year. Grampa reminded us that, except for the turkey, most of the food before us came from our land and from our labor. Without God, Grampa explained, this harvest would be impossible. Then we sat down to a feast containing all the colors of the rainbow.

Golden Brown Turkey

•

Bubbling-Hot Giblet Gravy

•

Baked Hubbard Squash

•

Whipped Mashed Potatoes

•

Green String Beans Seasoned
with Bacon Fat

•

Tossed Green Salad

•

Homemade Rolls

•

Celery and Olives

•

Homemade Finger Pickles

•

Christmas Cole Slaw

•

Mystery Fruitcake

•

Homemade Apricot Ice Cream

Unstuffed Turkey

Use a 20-lb. turkey. If frozen, thaw turkey for 3 to 4 days in refrigerator or for 8 to 10 hours in cold water.

Sprinkle inside of turkey, using salt and pepper. With a paper towel, rub inside with generous amount of shortening or butter. Insert a medium-sized onion.

Preheat oven to 325° F. and place turkey in pan and cover. Cook for 5 hours, basting every hour with giblet broth. Remove cover 30 minutes before turkey is done to allow browning. When done, remove turkey from oven and place on platter.

Stuffed Turkey

Use a 20-lb. turkey. Preheat oven to 325° F. Place turkey in pan and cover. Cook for 6 to 7 hours. Baste turkey every 2 hours, using giblet broth. Remove cover 1 hour before turkey is done to allow browning. When done, remove turkey from oven and place on platter.

Turkey Dressing

20 slices white bread
1   lb. ground sausage meat
1   stick butter
1½ cups chopped onion
1   cup finely chopped celery
1   cup finely chopped green peppers
½   cup chopped parsley
2   tsps. crumbled leaf sage
1½ cups giblet broth
4   eggs
    salt and pepper to taste

Toast bread and dice into cubes. Cook sausage meat, breaking up all lumps. Do not brown.

Pour off fat. Add sausage to bread cubes. Melt butter in a skillet. Add onion, celery, green peppers. Cook until onion shrivels. Stir constantly. Add bread mixture, salt, pepper, parsley, and sage. Moisten dressing with giblet broth. Break eggs and beat them lightly. Stir eggs into mixture. Stuff mixture into turkey.

Bubbling-Hot Giblet Gravy

Save 2 cups of giblet broth for basting turkey and for moistening turkey dressing.

Place turkey giblets, neck, heart, and gizzards in a large saucepan. Add 3 chicken bouillon cubes and 2 stalks of diced celery. Add water to level 2 inches above giblets.

Bring water to boil and let simmer for 2 hours. Pour off 2 cups of broth. Strain mixture, add pepper, and thicken to gravy.

Baked Hubbard Squash

6   lbs. Hubbard squash
4   tsps. salt
2   tsps. nutmeg
½   cup brown sugar
1   stick butter

Slice squash into halves. Remove seeds, wash squash, and cut into individual servings. Sprinkle each piece with salt, nutmeg, and brown sugar. Place a pat of butter on each piece. Place pieces in casserole, cover, and bake in 350°F. oven for 1 hour or until tender.

Green String Beans Seasoned with Bacon Fat

4 lbs. fresh string beans
3 chicken bouillon cubes
2 T. bacon fat

Place 3 cups of water, bouillon cubes, and bacon fat in saucepan and bring to a boil. Wash string beans, remove ends, and break beans into 2-inch lengths. Add string beans to water and simmer for 1 hour or until tender.

Homemade Finger Pickles

This delicacy we children prepared for Christmas dinner over sixty years ago. Preparation was done one week before Christmas with our promises not to get in the grownups' way and not to become a nuisance in the kitchen. We were so well-behaved, even Santa was pleased.

12 young cucumbers
6 small onions
½ cup salt
2 cups vinegar
½ cup sugar
2 tsps. mustard seed
2 tsps. celery seed
2 tsps. black pepper
1 tsp. ginger
1 tsp. turmeric

Slice cucumbers lengthwise into 8 strips, then each strip into quarters. Slice onions to size wanted. Add 1/2 cup salt, cover with water, and let stand for 2 hours. Drain solution, add other ingredients, and bring to boil. (Avoid making pickles soft.) Pack while hot in clean glass jars and seal immediately. Open for Christmas dinner.

These homemade finger pickles can be nibbled and snacked without spoiling appetites for Christmas dinner. Have a Merry Christmas!

Christmas Cole Slaw
Phyllis Walk

Uncle Will was a consistent winner of blue ribbons at the state fair for his cabbages. Every year, he would carefully choose two or three of his best heads in a crock in the root cellar to save for Christmas. Aunt Nell would make this recipe, which would be served with cold turkey at a buffet and open house during the holidays. Uncle Will would always brag about how smart he was in storing produce and would enlarge upon the fact that his prize winners in September were "goodly fare."

Then one year Aunt Nell inadvertently discovered the cabbages had gotten limp and a bit dried out, so she sneaked off to the supermarket to buy some to take their place.

As she was down in the cellar making the switch, in came Uncle Will with cabbage from the store to do the same thing! How they laughed and fell into each other's arms over the deception.

Now, each year after the fair, they use up the cabbage while it is fresh and buy new for the holidays. Uncle Will insists on having Christmas Slaw every year. "It is a symbol of how a good wife will protect her husband's self-esteem, even if he's got an ego bigger than the cabbages he grows," says Uncle Will. "And what greater gift can a man have than that!"

3 cups shredded green cabbage
3 cups shredded red cabbage
2 green peppers, seeded and diced
¼ cup chopped red Bermuda onion or
6 green onions, chopped, including tops
Mix with:
1 cup sour cream
¾ tsp. dill weed
½ tsp. salt

Toss thoroughly and serve 6 to 8.

CHRISTMAS DESSERTS

Steamed Fig Pudding
Sheryl Lazzarotti

In Texas, where figs grow in abundance, this is a favorite recipe. It brings to life the Christmas carol, "We Wish You a Merry Christmas, and Lots of Figgy Pudding."

Preheat oven to 325°F.
Beat until soft:
½ **cup butter**
½ **cup shortening**
Add, gradually:
1 **cup sugar**
3 **egg yolks, beaten (reserve the egg whites)**
1 **cup milk**
2 **T. imitation brandy flavoring**
Put through a grinder or chop:
1 **lb. dried figs (or more)**
1 **apple, peeled and cored**
Add:
   sprinkles of candied lemon and orange peel
1 **cup chopped pecans**
2 **tsps. granted orange rind**
½ **tsp. cinnamon**
⅛ **tsp. cloves**
⅛ **tsp. powdered ginger**
1½ **cups dried bread crumbs**
2 **tsps. baking powder**

Whip until stiff reserved egg whites, and fold into mixture. Pour into a greased oven-proof bowl and steam slowly for 4 hours. Serve with a hot Sabayon sauce. Serves 14.

Homemade Apricot Ice Cream
Oscar Greene

1 **16-oz. can apricots**
2 **cups sugar**
¼ **cup lemon juice**
   few grains salt
2 **quarts heavy cream**

Puree apricots through potato masher. Mix together sugar, lemon juice, and salt. Add apricot juice, puree, and cream. Stir mixture.

Use 2-gallon hand ice-cream freezer. Place freezer can in tub. Fill can two thirds. (Mixture will expand during freezing.) Insert dasher, slip on cover, and install crank and handle. Fill tub one third with ice. Add alternate layers of salt and crushed ice to top of can. Pack down and let stand for 5 minutes. Then turn handle slowly for 5 to 10 minutes. Add salt and crushed ice as needed. Turn handle rapidly until turning becomes difficult. Clear ice and salt from cover. (DO NOT ALLOW SALT TO SEEP INTO ICE CREAM!) Remove crank and handle. Lift off cover and pull out dasher. Cover can with waxed paper. Replace cover. Repack tub with crushed ice and salt. Cover with rug and blanket. Store in cool place until time for serving. Ice cream will remain firm 2 to 3 hours.

Mystery Fruitcake
Phyllis Walk

The mystery about this fruitcake is how it tastes so good yet is so easy to prepare. Mother always served as chairperson of the church Christmas bazaar and didn't always have time to prepare the traditional complicated recipes she usually enjoyed doing. But she still wanted to give fruitcake as gifts or have some around the house to nibble, and this was an ingenious way of doing it all.

1   package store-bought spice cake mix

Bake according to directions; cool and crumble cake into a large bowl. Add to the crumbs and mix well the following:

4   cups mixed glazed fruit
½   cup green candied cherries
¼   cup red candied cherries
1½   cups raisins
1   cup chopped dates
4½   cups chopped pecans

Now add 1 package fluffy frosting mix made according to box instructions. Knead and blend well with hands and pack very firmly into 2 foil-lined bread pans. Refrigerate until ready to slice and serve or to wrap to give as gifts.

Mama's Hard-Times Fruitcake
Doris C. Crandall

During the dust-bowl days, my family lived in the Texas panhandle. Many of our neighbors gave up and moved to California, but Daddy chose to stick to the land. When I couldn't have something I wanted, Mama would say, "Times are hard. Maybe we'll make a crop next year."

Although we had few cakes during those years, Mama always managed to have her hard-times fruitcake for Chrismas. It was extra special then and still is. Mama put plenty of icing between the layers to make it sweet and gooey. Oh yes, Aunt Kate, Mama's sister, sent us the pecans. They grew wild on her East Texas farm.

2   cups sugar
¾   cup shortening
1   tsp. soda
1   cup buttermilk
¼   tsp. cloves
1   tsp. cinnamon
1   tsp. allspice
2½   cups sifted flour
1   tsp. baking powder
3   eggs
1   cup prunes, cooked, pitted, and mashed
1   cup chopped pecans

Cream sugar and shortening.
Dissolve soda in buttermilk.
Sift together spices, flour, and baking powder and add to sugar mixture alternately with buttermilk.
Add beaten eggs, prunes, and pecans.
Bake in three 9-inch greased and floured cake pans in 350°F. oven until toothpick inserted in middle comes out clean.

Icing:
1½   cups brown sugar
½   cup sweet cream

Boil sugar and cream until threads. Cool slightly.
Beat until thick.
Extra prunes and pecans may be added to the icing.

CHRISTMAS COOKIES

Spritz Cookies
Peggy Brooke

1 lb. butter
1 cup sugar
2 eggs
4 cups flour
1 tsp. vanilla

Mix in the above order. Push through a cookie press or drop by teaspoonfuls on a cookie sheet. Bake at 400°F., 8 to 10 minutes.

Peanut Butter Cookies
Janet Shaffer

1 lb. margarine
1 lb. peanut butter (2 cups)
1 lb. sugar (2 cups)
1 lb. brown sugar (2 cups, packed)
4 eggs
1 T. vanilla
1 T. baking soda
2 tsps. salt
5 cups all-purpose flour

Mix ingredients in order given. Using a tablespoon, place cookies on a greased baking sheet. Bake 10 to 12 minutes at 350°F. Makes 100 cookies.

Oatmeal-Nut Cookies
Marjorie Lindsey Brewer

1 cup sugar
¼ cup vegetable oil
1 tsp. vanilla
2 eggs
4 Tbs. sweet milk
2 cups oatmeal
2 cups flour
1 tsp. baking powder
1 tsp. cinnamon
1 cup raisins
1 cup nuts

Mix sugar, vegetable oil, and vanilla. Stir in slightly beaten eggs, milk, and oatmeal. While stirring, sift in flour, with baking powder and cinnamon added. Add raisins and nuts. Drop spoonfuls of the mixture onto a greased cookie pan. Bake at 350°F., 8 to 10 minutes.

Tea-Time Chocolate Puffs
Terri Castillo

½ cup shortening
1⅔ cups sugar
2 eggs
2 oz. baking chocolate
½ cup broken pecans
2½ cups sifted flour
2 tsps. baking powder
½ tsp. salt
⅓ cup milk
2 tsps. vanilla
1 confectioners sugar

Thoroughly cream together shortening and sugar. Add beaten eggs and chocolate that has been melted over low heat. Stir in pecans. Sift dry ingredients together and add alternately with milk that has been flavored with vanilla. Cover and chill for 3 hours.

Before shaping, heat oven to 350°F. Form dough into 1-inch balls, then roll in confectioners sugar.

Bake on cookie sheet in 350°F. oven for 10 minutes. Yields 60 cookies.

CHRISTMAS
CANDIES AND NUTS

Seven-Layer Squares
Betty R. Schneider

1   stick butter
1   cup graham cracker crumbs
3½ oz. shredded coconut
1   cup coarsely broken walnuts
1   6-oz. package chocolate chips
1   6-oz. package butterscotch chips
1   can sweetened condensed milk

Melt butter in 9 x 13-in. dish or pan. Mix in the graham cracker crumbs and spread to cover bottom of dish. Sprinkle the coconut over butter and crumb mixture. Then spread walnuts over the above. Sprinkle chocolate and butterscotch chips over all. Pour the condensed milk from corner to corner of dish, making certain that each square inch is covered. Bake in 350°F. oven for 25 minutes. Cool. Cut into squares.

Choco-Nut Bonbons
Virginia Westervelt

1   cup butter or margarine, softened
1   15-oz. can sweetened condensed milk
2   lbs. powdered sugar
2   14-oz. boxes flaked coconut
1   lb. walnuts or pecans, finely chopped
3   6-oz. packages chocolate chips
1   block (¼ lb.) household paraffin

Mix together butter, condensed milk, sugar, coconut, and nuts. Roll into small balls. Place on cookie sheet and chill. Melt chocolate pieces and paraffin together in saucepan on *warm* or in a double boiler. Place a toothpick in each candy ball, dip in warm chocolate mixture, and replace on cookie sheet for chocolate to harden. Refrigerate or freeze until needed. Yield: 250 bonbons.

"You-Got-Chocolate-On-My-Peanut-Butter" Candy
Sue Monk Kidd

12 oz. peanut butter
1   lb. confectioners sugar
1½ sticks butter (soft)
2   large-size chocolate bars

Mix together on medium speed peanut butter, sugar, and butter, and spread in a 9 x 13-in. pan. Melt chocolate bars over low heat, stirring constantly. Smooth over pressed mixture. Refrigerate. When cooled, cut into squares.

Peanut Butter Pinwheels
Betty R. Graham

1   lb. confectioners sugar, sifted
¼   lb. butter, softened
      milk
½   tsp. vanilla
      peanut butter

In a large bowl, sift confectioners sugar over softened butter, reserving about ½ cup of sugar for the rolling process. Cream butter and confectioners sugar, adding milk, a few drops at a time, until the mixture sticks together to a consistency that can be rolled. Add vanilla; mix and form into a large ball. Divide fondant in two parts. Sprinkle confectioners sugar on pastry sheet or waxed paper and rolling pin. Roll each ball to ¼-in. thickness. Spread generously with peanut butter. Roll up jelly-roll fashion. Sprinkle more sugar on sheet and roll with both hands until the roll is about 1 in. in diameter. With a sharp knife, slice roll into bite-sized pieces. Store in the refrigerator.

Pecan Tassies
Drue Duke

Pastry:
3 oz. cream cheese, softened
½ cup butter or margarine
1 cup sifted, plain flour

Blend cream cheese and butter or margarine. Stir in flour. Chill for about 1 hour. Shape into 24 1-in. balls. Place in 1¾-inch muffin tins. Press dough against sides and bottom.

Filling:
1 egg
¾ cup brown sugar
1 T. soft butter or margarine
1 tsp. vanilla extract
    dash of salt
⅓ cup coarsely broken pecans

Beat together egg, sugar, butter, vanilla, and salt until smooth. Divide half of the pecans among pastry-lined cups. Spoon in egg mixture on top of pecans. Sprinkle remaining pecans on egg mixture. Bake in slow oven at 325°F. for 25 minutes or until filling is set. Cool and remove from pan. Makes 24.

Cream Candy
Janet Shaffer

2 cups sugar
2 T. vinegar
1 tsp. cream of tartar
1 tsp. lemon extract

Add a little water to moisten the sugar; boil with vinegar and cream of tartar, without stirring, until brittle when tried in cold water. Add lemon extract; turn out quickly on buttered plate. When cool enough to handle, pull until white and cut into small pieces.

Penuche
Janet Shaffer

2 cups light brown sugar
⅓ cup milk
1 T. butter
¾ cup chopped nuts
1 tsp. vanilla extract

Put sugar, milk, and butter into saucepan. Boil with as little stirring as possible until it makes a soft ball in cold water. Take from fire, add nuts and vanilla, beat until thick, and pour into greased pans.

Nutty Squares
Betty R. Schneider

1 cup white sugar
1 cup white corn syrup
1 cup chunk-style peanut butter
6 cups toasted flakes cereal
1 6-oz. package chocolate chips
1 6-oz. package butterscotch chips

Combine sugar and syrup in top of double boiler and bring almost to a boil. Add peanut butter. Continue cooking until well mixed. Do *not* bring to boil (approx. 1 minute).

Spread 6 cups of cereal in 9 x 13-in. flat pan. Pour the cooked mixture over cereal and mix thoroughly. Pat with spatula to flatten evenly.

Melt the chocolate and butterscotch chips in top of double boiler. Frost the top of cereal mixture with this. Refrigerate. Within an hour or two, cut in 1-in. squares.

Italian Chestnuts
Terri Castillo

1 lb. bag of chestnuts

Make 2 crosscut gashes on the flat side of each chestnut shell, using a sharp, pointed knife. Cover chestnuts with boiling water and cook for 15 minutes. Drain and remove skins. Do not overcook. Break chestnuts in half, keeping pieces as large as possible.

CHRISTMAS DRINKS

Mari's Egg Nog
Mari Elam

For 1½ qts.:
6   eggs
1   cup sugar
¾   tsp. salt
    rum flavoring (just add till it tastes right)
1½   quarts light cream (I use ½ evaporated milk and ½ water)

Beat eggs till light and foamy. Add sugar and salt, beating until thick and well blended. Stir in rum flavoring and cream. Chill at least 3 hours. Sprinkle with nutmeg before serving.

Christmas Punch
Pat King

My favorite punch that brightens up the Christmas meal table!

2   large bottles ginger ale
1   large can Hawaiian Punch
1   large can orange punch drink
1   small bottle Real Lemon
6   packages Kool-Aid (red)
2   gallons water
8   cups sugar

Stir in pre-chilled punch bowl.

Christmas Egg Nog
Ruth Ritchie

My husband is noted far and wide for his very delicious and wickedly rich egg nog. It's a recipe he developed himself over several years of experimenting.

1   dozen eggs
¾   cup sugar
2   quarts milk
*1 quart heavy cream
1   pint vanilla ice cream
    ground nutmeg

*Heavy cream ought to be a few days old for better whipping:

The day before serving—separate eggs and beat yolks with sugar until thick and lemony.

Stir in milk and chill overnight.

Prior to serving, beat egg whites until stiff and fold into prechilled mixture.

Whip heavy cream until stiff and place in the bottom of a prechilled punch bowl. Add prechilled milk-egg mixture. Add vanilla ice cream. It helps to keep the eggnog cold, as well as adding flavor. Sprinkle nutmeg over the top.

Yield: 4 quarts.

INDEX

All illustrations are copyright © by the photographers and artists listed below.

Many thanks to:

Sonja Bullaty and Angelo Lomeo for photographs on pages: 2, 5, 23, 25 (top), 35, 36 (top), 37, 40 (bottom), 41 (top), 46, 48, 50, 53, 85, 95, 110, 113, 124, 129, 134 (bottom), 139, 144, 147, 148, 151, 152, 167 (right), 170, 171 (top), 176, 192.

Hanson Carroll for the photographs on pages: 11, 32 (top), 136.

Carol Fiorino for the illustrations on pages: 42, 78–79, 81, 106, 168, 187.

Wendy Frost for the illustrations on pages: 34, 54, 57, 59, 61, 64, 67, 68, 128, 153, 154, 155, 157, 158, 159, 161.

Steven Fuller for the photograph, "Lodgepole pine tree on rimrock at sunrise, Yellowstone Park," on page 173.

Robert LoGrippo for the art on pages: 17, 18, 19.

Preston Lyon for photographs on pages: 22 (top), 29, 88, 91, 108.

Judy Pelikan for the illustrations on pages: 10–11, 14–15, 20–21, 44–45, 70–72, 74–75, 104–105, 132–133, 162–164, 174–175.

Lilo Raymond for her photographs on pages: 39, 40 (top), 87, 123, 130, 141, 142, 165, 167 (left). Photographs on pages: 12, 76, 84, 94, 119, 120, 126, 131, 134 (top), 169, 179 used with permission of Ladies Home Journal.

Don Warning for his extraordinary collection of Victorian art on pages: 3, 4, 13, 25 (right), 26, 27, 31, 33, 36 (bottom), 38, 41 (bottom), 43, 92, 96, 98–103, 107, 121, 122, 125, 137, 138, 140, 143, 150, 166, 171 (bottom), 172, 183.